Kids Learn!

Review Fourth Grade
Get Ready for Fifth Grade

Editor-in-Chief	**Creative Director**
Sharon Coan, M.S.Ed.	Lee Aucoin
Editorial Manager	**Imaging**
Gisela Lee, M.A.	Phil Garcia
	Sandra Riley
Editors	Misty Shaw
Jenni Corcoran, M.A.Ed.	
Maria Elvira Gallardo, M.A.	**Cover Artist**
Wanda Kelly, M.A.	Lee Aucoin
Kathy Knoblock, M.A.Ed.	
Jodene Smith, M.A.Ed.	**Publisher**
	Corinne Burton, M.A.Ed.

Beach City Press
5301 Oceanus Drive
Huntington Beach, CA 92649
www.beachcitypress.com
ISBN-1-4258-0119-6

©2007 Beach City Press, Inc.
Made in U.S.A.

Table of Contents/Índice de materias

Useful Ideas and Suggestions for Parents

Ideas y sugerencias útiles para padres

Things to Do at Home

To Practice Reading

- Send your child on a "Print Hunt." Challenge the child to find as many different types of print matter in your home as he or she can (e.g., labels, directions, maps, etc.).

- Have your child find four different ads in a magazine and identify the target audience for each.

- After reading a short story or a newspaper article, ask your child to retell the events in order using the words First, Next, Then, and Finally.

- Invite your child to read and follow a recipe to make a family dish or dessert.

To Practice Writing

- Have your child listen carefully to a television or radio commercial. Ask him or her to write at least one fact and opinion he or she heard.

- Let your child use a TV schedule to find an educational program on a topic in which he or she is interested. Have the child practice taking notes during the show. Then, following the program, have him or her write a summary paragraph about it.

- Ask your child to record everything he or she eats in one day, and then write about any observations and conclusions drawn from this activity.

- Using a newspaper or magazine article, challenge your child to find and list all the words that have prefixes. You can repeat this exercise each week by changing the challenge to another word pattern, such as words with suffixes, words with silent letters, words with three syllables, words that are synonyms for said, words that are proper nouns, and so on.

- Have your child use a newspaper to find examples of writing for three different purposes: to inform, to entertain, and to persuade. Then, have him or her choose a topic and write a paragraph about it with each of the purposes (e.g., topic pigs. to inform: the characteristics of pigs; to entertain: a story about a pig who thought he was a dog; to persuade: why people should not eat ham and bacon).

To Practice Math

- Have your child divide a whole food product into the number of servings suggested on the label, and then answer these questions: 1. How accurate is the proposed serving size compared with reality? 2. How many calories would be in the portion you would eat in a serving?

- Ask your child to calculate the area of his or her room. Then, challenge him or her to find the area of every room in the house and make a graph of the results.

- If you have a pet, have your child determine how long a bag of food will last based on the amount you feed each day. If you have the price of the bag available, have the child calculate the cost per day as well. (If you do not have a pet, you could do this activity with something your family uses regularly, such as laundry detergent.)

- Have your child estimate the weight of several objects around the house. (To make it more fun and engaging, do this along with your child!). Then, show your child how to find the actual weight of the object by weighing himself or herself both with and without the object and then subtracting the difference.

Cosas para hacer en casa

Para practicar la lectura

- Envíe a su hijo o hija a "La caza de cosas impresas". Desafíelo a encontrar en casa la mayor cantidad de materiales impresos de distintos tipos que sea posible. (p. ej. etiquetas, instrucciones, mapas,…)

- Pídale a su hijo que encuentre cuatro anuncios distintos en una revista y que identifique el público al que está dirigido cada uno.

- Después de leer un cuento corto o artículo del periódico, pídale a su hijo que le vuelva a contar lo que sucedió en orden usando las palabras Primero, Luego, Después y Por último.

- Invite a su hijo a leer y seguir una receta para hacer una comida o postre para la familia.

Para practicar la escritura

- Pídale a su hijo que escuche atentamente un anuncio de radio o televisión. Pídale que escriba al menos un hecho y una opinión que haya escuchado.

- Pídale a su hijo que use la programación de los canales de TV para encontrar un programa educativo sobre un tema que le interese. Pídale a su hijo que practique tomar notas durante el programa. Después del programa, pídale que escriba un párrafo de resumen.

- Pídale a su hijo que lleve un registro de todo lo que come en un día, y después que escriba cualquier observación o conclusión que surja de esta actividad.

- Con un artículo de periódico o de revista, desafíe a su hijo a encontrar y enumerar todas las palabras que contengan prefijos. Pueden repetir este ejercicio todas las semanas cambiando el desafío a otro tipo de palabra, como palabras con sufijos, con letras mudas, de tres sílabas, que son sinónimos de "decir", que son sustantivos propios, y así sucesivamente.

- Pídale a su hijo que use un periódico para encontrar ejemplos de tres objetivos distintos: informar, entretener o persuadir. Después, pídale que elija un tema y escriba un párrafo al respecto con cada uno de esos objetivos. (e.g., tema "los cerdos". para informar: las características de los cerdos; para entretener: un cuento sobre un cerdo que creía que era un perro; para persuadir: por qué la gente no debería comer jamón y tocino)

Para practicar las matemáticas

- Pídale a su hijo que divida un producto alimenticio entero en la cantidad de porciones sugeridas en la etiqueta, y luego que responda a estas preguntas: 1. ¿Qué nivel de exactitud hay entre la porción propuesta y la realidad? 2. ¿Cuántas calorías tendría la porción que tú comerías?

- Pídale a su hijo que calcule el área de su habitación. Después, desafíelo a averiguar el área de todas las habitaciones de la casa. Pídale que haga una gráfica con los resultados.

- Si tiene una mascota, pídale a su hijo que calcule cuánto durará una bolsa de comida según la cantidad que se le da cada día. Si sabe el precio de la bolsa, pídale a su hijo que calcule el costo por día también. (Si no tienen una mascota, hagan esta actividad con algo que la familia use regularmente, como jabón para la ropa.)

- Pídale a su hijo que estime el peso de varios objetos de la casa. (Para que sea más divertido e interesante, ¡hágalo usted también!) Después, muéstrele a su hijo cómo averiguar el peso exacto de cada objeto pesándose uno mismo con y sin el objeto, y luego restando.

Things to Do in the Community

To Practice Reading

- On a trip to somewhere new, have your child navigate by reading a map.

- Have your child find out what hours your nearest public library is open and what special programs or activities it sponsors for kids. (Also, check out bookstores, which sometimes have contests or other reading incentives directed for various ages of children.)

- Set aside a regular time each week for a "Read-Aloud." At this time have your child read to a younger sibling or neighbor, choose something to read aloud and discuss with you, or read something to your child that would interest him or her and then talk about it.

- Let your child choose a "pet plant" to care for from a local nursery or home improvement store. Have him or her select the plant based on reading the information about what the different plants need to survive and thrive.

- Have your child read the community section of the newspaper or a church or community newsletter. Ask him or her to select topics of interest to share with the family.

To Practice Writing

- Give your child a small notebook and let him or her choose what kind of journal to keep in it—personal, travel, observations, interesting quotes, ideas for future consideration? (If your child wants to keep the journal private, be sure to respect his or her wishes.)

- Ask your child to come up with ways he or she can earn spending money. Then have him or her design and write an ad that sells his or her service or product, such as babysitting or grocery shopping for someone housebound. Remind your child that an ad must appeal to the people who want to buy, clearly explain the product or service, and give details of what it will cost the buyer and why he or she should spend the money (the advantage for the buyer).

- Have your child locate your community fire station. Then, let him or her visit, call, or write for information about fire safety. Ask him or her to design and write a fire escape plan for your family.

- Work with your child to make a family tree. Then, have your child write a letter to a relative explaining what he or she is doing. He or she could then ask for missing information in the tree, introduce himself or herself if they have never met, or ask the relative to tell what another relative he or she knew was like.

To Practice Math

- Have your child compare gas prices at three different stations for two weeks, and then calculate the cost of filling up the family vehicle at each station to determine which is the best value.

- Many fast food restaurants have nutritional information sheets. Ask your child to pick up one, and then use it to calculate the total calories/fat of various combinations of foods he or she might eat there.

- According to County of Los Angeles Department of Public Works, "Each of us generates on average 4.4 pounds of waste per day per person." Make up word problems that revolve around this statement (e.g., how many days would it take to generate your weight in waste?). For extra motivation, do the calculations yourself along side your child.

- Give your child the amount of your food budget for a week. Have him or her determine the average daily cost of feeding the family for a week. Then, invite your child to go to the grocery store with you and compare prices of brand names vs. store brands and large quantities vs. smaller quantities. Ask your child to help you select items that are the best value for the money.

Cosas para hacer en la comunidad

Para Practicar la lectura

- En un viaje a un lugar nuevo, pídale a su hijo que ayude leyendo el mapa.

- Pídale a su hijo que averigüe el horario de la biblioteca local más cercana y qué programas o actividades especiales ofrecen para niños. (También consulte en librerías, que a veces tienen concursos u otros incentivos para la lectura dirigidos a niños de distintas edades.)

- Fije un horario regular todas las semanas para "Leer en voz alta". En el tiempo dispuesto, pídale a su hijo que le lea a un hermano más pequeño o vecino, que elija algo para leer en voz alta y comentar con usted, o lea usted algo que sea del interés del niño y que puedan comentar después.

- Pídale a su hijo que elija una "planta mascota" para cuidar en el vivero local o la tienda. Pídale que elija la planta de acuerdo a la información de lo que las distintas plantas necesitan para sobrevivir y crecer.

- Pídale a su hijo que lea la sección de la comunidad del periódico o el boletín de la comunidad o la iglesia. Pídale que elija temas de interés para compartir con la familia.

Para practicar la escritura

- Déle a su hijo o hija un cuaderno pequeño y permítale elegir qué tipo de diario va a llevar: personal, de viaje, observaciones, citas interesantes, ideas para el futuro, etc. (Si su hijo quiere que el diario sea privado, respete sus deseos.)

- Pídale a su hijo que proponga maneras en que puede ganar dinero para gastar. Después pídale que diseñe y escriba un aviso donde venda su producto o servicio, como cuidar niños o hacer las compras para personas que no pueden salir de su casa. Recuérdele que un aviso debe ser atractivo para la gente que uno desea como cliente, que debe explicar claramente el producto o servicio, y que debe dar detalles sobre el costo y las razones por las que deberían gastar ese dinero (la ventaja para el cliente).

- Pídale a su hijo que ubique la estación de bomberos de la comunidad. Después, permítale visitar, llamar o escribir pidiendo información sobre la prevención de incendios. Pídale que diseñe y escriba un plan de escape ante incendios para la familia.

- Trabaje con su hijo para hacer un árbol genealógico. Después, pídale que escriba una carta a un pariente y le explique lo que está haciendo. Le puede pedir información que necesite para el árbol, presentarse si no se conocen, o preguntarle cómo era algún otro pariente que conozca.

Para practicar las matemáticas

- Pídale a su hijo o hija que compare el precio de la gasolina en tres estaciones distintas durante dos semanas, y después calcule el costo de llenar el tanque del vehículo de la familia en cada una para determinar cuál es el mejor valor.

- Muchos restaurantes de comida rápida tienen hojas de información nutricional. Pídale a su hijo que tome una y luego la use para calcular la cantidad total de calorías/grasa de distintas combinaciones de comidas que se ofrecen allí.

- Según el Departamento de Obras Públicas del condado de Los Ángeles, "cada uno de nosotros genera un promedio de 4.4 libras de basura por día". Inventen problemas escritos alrededor de esta afirmación (por ejemplo, ¿cuántos días tomará generar tu propio peso en basura?) Si desea mayor motivación, haga usted también los cálculos junto con su hijo.

- Dígale a su hijo el importe de su presupuesto para alimentos de una semana. Pídale que determine el costo promedio diario de alimentar a la familia una semana. Después, invite a su hijo a ir a la tienda con usted y comparar los precios de las marcas conocidas con las marcas de la tienda, y cantidades mayores con cantidades más reducidas. Pídale a su hijo que le ayude a elegir artículos que ofrezcan el mejor valor por su dinero.

Introduction to Vacation Reading

The next page provides a list of recommended literature for children and adolescents in grades 4 and 5. The titles listed are recommendations for vacation reading for your child. The list includes both fiction and nonfiction books so that your child will experience a wide variety of types of reading similar to what he or she experiences in the classroom.

In each group of pages within this book, your child will be asked to select a book to read and to complete an activity related to that book. This list will provide some guidance in making those selections. These are only suggestions, however. If your child chooses other reading material, that is fine. Children will be more likely to read what they have chosen themselves.

Visits to your local library so your child can choose books to read will prove invaluable in helping your child maintain the gains in reading that have been made over the past year. Make sure your child chooses books that are at a reading level that is comfortable for him or her. If the books on this list seem too hard or too easy for your child, ask the librarian for guidance in choosing books that are leveled appropriately.

Most of all, make sure your child has chosen books that are interesting to him or her. Vacation reading should be fun!

Introducción a la lectura de las vacaciones

La siguiente página proporciona una lista de literatura recomendada para niños y adolescentes en 4° y 5° grado. Los títulos enumerados son sugerencias de literatura para las vacaciones. La lista comprende tanto libros de ficción como de no ficción para que su hijo o hija experimente con una amplia variedad de tipos de lectura, similar a la que se le ofrece en el salón de clase.

En cada juego de páginas de este libro, su hijo deberá seleccionar un libro para leer y completar una actividad relacionada. Esta lista sirve como guía para elegir una lectura, sin embargo, se trata sólo de sugerencias. Si su hijo prefiere otro material de lectura, está bien. Es más probable que los niños lean lo que han elegido por sí mismos.

Las visitas a la biblioteca local para que su hijo pueda elegir libros qué leer son una ayuda invaluable para ayudarlo a mantener los avances logrados durante el año anterior. Asegúrese de que su hijo elija libros con un nivel de lectura con el que se sienta cómodo. Si los libros de la lista resultan muy difíciles o muy fáciles para su hijo, pídale al bibliotecario que les ayude a elegir libros del nivel correcto.

Lo más importante, es asegurar de que su hijo haya elegido libros que sean de su interés. ¡La lectura durante las vacaciones debe de ser divertida!

Suggested Vacation Reading

These books are recommended for students in grades 4 and 5. Most, if not all, of these books are available at your local library or bookstore.

Estos libros son recomendados para estudiantes de 4° y 5° grado. La mayoría de estos libros, sino todos, están disponibles en su biblioteca local o librería.

Grade 4

Author	Title
King-Smith, Dick	*Babe: The Galliant Pig*
Robinson, Barbara	*The Best Christmas Pageant Ever*
Dahl, Roald	*Charlie and the Chocolate Factory*
Fitzhugh, Louise	*Harriet the Spy*
Lord, Bette Bao	*In the Year of the Boar and Jackie Robinson*
Wilder, Laura Ingalls	*Little House on the Prairie*
Coerr, Eleanor	*Sadako and the Thousand Paper Cranes*
MacLachlan, Patricia	*Sarah, Plain and Tall*
Naylor, Phyllis	*Shiloh*
MacLachlan, Patricia	*Skylark*
Curtis, Christopher Paul	*The Watsons Go to Birmingham—1963*
Sachar, Louis	*Wayside School Is Falling Down*

Grade 5

Author	Title
Fleischman, Sid	*By the Great Horn Spoon*
Carson Levine, Gail	*Ella Enchanted*
Blos, Joan	*A Gathering of Days: A New England Girl's Journal*
Rowling, J.K.	*Harry Potter and the Sorcerer's Stone*
Uchida, Yoshiko	*Journey to Topaz*
Kipling, Rudyard	*The Jungle Book*
O'Brien, Robert	*Mrs. Frisby and the Rats of NIMH*
Hesse, Karen	*The Music of Dolphins*
Lowry, Lois	*Number the Stars*
Gipson, Fred	*Old Yeller*
Juster, Norton	*The Phantom Tollbooth*
Burnett, Frances Hodgson	*The Secret Garden*
Babbitt, Natalie	*Tuck Everlasting*

Reading Log

Help your child complete this reading log to keep track of his or her vacation reading.

Ayude a su hijo a completar este registro de lectura para llevar la cuenta de su lectura durante las vacaciones.

Date	Title	Number of Pages	Author

Websites for Parents and Kids

- Fact Monster
  http://www.factmonster.com/
  Atlas, almanacs, dictionary, thesaurus, world, U.S., people, and more

- Edupuppy
  http://www.edupuppy.com/index.htm
  Large database of pre-screened sites appropriate for kids and their families

- Children's Book Council
  http://www.cbcbooks.org/
  Tips for reading to young children and reading activities

- Book Adventure
  http://www.bookadventure.com/
  Book quizzes for many of the books found on the Suggested Vacation Reading list

- Read, Write, Think
  http://www.readwritethink.org/materials/in_the_bag/index.html
  Student materials that support literacy learning in the K–12 classroom

- Kidsource
  http://www.kidsource.com
  Activities for children from infancy to age 10

- Reading Rockets
  http://www.readingrockets.org/series.php
  Information, activities, and advice for parents

- ¡Colorín Colorado!
  http://www.colorincolorado.org/
  Information, activities, and advice for parents and educators of Spanish-speaking students

- Reading is Fundamental
  http://www.rif.org/parents/
  Ideas for parents to encourage reading at home

- Bookhive
  http://www.bookhive.org/
  Book reviews and recommendations

- Primary Computer Games
  http://www.primarygames.com/
  Educational computer games for elementary children

- Helping Your Child Learn Math
  http://www.ed.gov/pubs/parents/Math/index.html
  Math activities to do at home, at the grocery store, on the road, etc.

- Math Games
  http://www.mathplayground.com/index.html
  Math games for students in grades K–6

- Ask Dr. Math
  http://mathforum.org/dr.math/
  Question and answer service for math students and parents

- PBS Early Math
  http://www.pbs.org/parents/earlymath/grades_flash.html
  Math-based activities and developmental milestones for children from 6 to 9 years old

- Aunty Math
  http://www.dupagechildrensmuseum.org/aunty
  Real-life problem solving challenges appropriate for grades K–5

- Cool Math for Kids
  http://www.coolmath4kids.com/
  Math games, puzzles, calculators, etc.

- Figure This! Math Challenges for Families
  http://www.figurethis.org/
  Math problems to challenge families

- A+ Math
  http://www.aplusmath.com/Flashcards/
  Math flash cards for addition, subtraction, multiplication, and division

Spanish Websites for Students and Parents
Sitios web en español para los estudiantes y los padres

- Mundo Latino
  http://www.mundolatino.org/rinconcito
  Base de datos extensivo para personas que hablan español a nivel mundial con enlaces a todos los temas, de juegos educativos y revistas en la red.

- EduHound Español
  http://www.eduhound.com/espanol/
  Base de datos al día de más de 30,000 enlaces educativos en todos los temas

- StoryPlace
  http://www.storyplace.org/sp/storyplace.asp
  Lo último en la biblioteca digital de los niños. Explore estas páginas llenas de cuentos para niños, jóvenes y adultos.

- ¡Colorín Colorado!
  http://www.colorincolorado.org/
  Información, actividades y consejos para padres y maestros de estudiantes que hablan español

Reading Fluency

Reading fluency is the ability to read with accuracy and speed, as well as with proper expression.

Accuracy is the number of words that are read correctly. Accuracy develops as a result of many opportunities to practice reading with a considerable amount of success. Therefore, your child should read and reread text that contains mostly words he or she can read or decode easily. If your child misreads more than 1 out of every 10 words, the text is probably too difficult for him or her, even if assistance is provided.

Reading rate or speed is the rate at which a student can read a given text. Nonfluent readers will read slowly and deliberately, whereas fluent readers will read quickly and easily. One way to determine your child's reading rate is to calculate the number of words he or she can read correctly in one minute.

To determine your child's reading rate,

1. Select reading materials at the right level for your child.
2. Ask your child to read aloud for exactly one minute.
3. On a separate sheet of paper, make a note of any words your child misreads.
4. Count the total number of correct words your child reads in one minute.
5. The result is your child's reading rate or the number of words read correctly per minute (WPM).

Reading Fluency Chart

Grade	Reading Rate
1st	60 wpm
2nd	90 wpm
3rd	115 wpm
4th	130 wpm
5th+	145 wpm

Fluidez en la lectura

La fluidez en la lectura es la habilidad de leer con precisión y velocidad, utilizando además la entonación correcta.

La precisión es la cantidad de palabras leídas correctamente. Se desarrolla como resultado de muchas oportunidades de práctica de lectura con un grado considerable de éxito. Por lo tanto, su hijo o hija debe leer una y otra vez aquellos textos que contengan principalmente palabras que puede leer o descifrar fácilmente. Si su hijo se equivoca más de 1 vez cada 10 palabras, posiblemente el texto sea demasiado difícil, incluso si se le brinda asistencia.

La velocidad de lectura es la velocidad con la cual el estudiante puede leer un texto dado. Los lectores que no tienen fluidez leerán de forma lenta y deliberada, mientras que los lectores con fluidez leerán rápidamente y fácilmente. Una manera de determinar la velocidad de lectura de su hijo es calcular la cantidad de palabras que lee correctamente en un minuto.

Para determinar la velocidad de lectura,

1. Seleccione material de lectura del nivel correcto para su hijo.
2. Pídale a su hijo que lea en voz alta exactamente por un minuto.
3. En una hoja aparte, anote cuantas palabras lee mal.
4. Cuente el total de palabras correctas que su hijo leyó en un minuto.
5. El resultado es la velocidad de lectura o la cantidad de palabras leídas correctamente por minuto (PPM).

Tabla de Fluidez en la Lectura

Grado	Velocidad de Lectura
1°	60 ppm
2°	90 ppm
3°	115 ppm
4°	130 ppm
5°+	145 ppm

Strategies for Fluency Practice

Read Alouds

To read fluently, your child must first hear what fluent reading sounds like. One of the best ways for you to help your child become a more fluent reader is to read aloud to him or her often and with great expression. Carefully choose the books you read to your child. Make sure you select a wide variety of genres, including fiction, nonfiction, poetry, nursery rhymes, and folk and fairy tales. Also, read books that will spark your child's interests and draw him or her into the reading experience.

Model Reading

Have your child select a book on his or her reading level. First read aloud to your child, providing him or her with a model of fluent reading, while he or she follows along in the book. Then your child should read aloud the same book while you provide assistance and encouragement.

Choral Reading

Select a book on your child's reading level. Read aloud to your child and invite him or her to join in as he or she recognizes the words. Continue to read and reread the book, encouraging your child to read along with you. Your child should read the book with you several times. After the third or fourth reading, your child should be able to read the text independently.

Estrategias para practicar la fluidez

Lectura en voz alta

Para poder leer con fluidez, los niños deben antes escuchar cómo es una lectura fluida. Una de las mejores maneras en que puede ayudarles a leer con más fluidez es leer en voz alta a menudo y con gran entonación. Elija cuidadosamente los libros que lee a su hijo. Asegúrese de elegir una amplia variedad de géneros, donde se incluya la ficción, no ficción, poesía, versos infantiles, y cuentos folclóricos y de hadas. También lea libros que despierten el interés de su hijo y lo atraigan a la experiencia de la lectura.

Lectura modelo

Haga que su hijo elija un libro en su nivel de lectura. Primero léaselo en voz alta, a modo de modelo de lectura fluida, mientras su hijo le sigue en el libro. Después, su hijo debe leer en voz alta el mismo libro, con su ayuda y aliento.

Lectura al mismo tiempo

Elija un libro del nivel de lectura de su hijo. Léaselo en voz alta e invite a su hijo a unírsele a medida que reconoce las palabras. Continúe leyendo el libro una y otra vez, alentando a su hijo a leer con usted. Su hijo tendrá que leer el libro con usted varias veces. Después de la tercera o cuarta vez, su hijo debe poder leer el texto de manera independiente.

Glossary

A

acute angle: an angle that measures less than 90 degrees

adjective: a word that describes a noun or pronoun

adverb: a word that describes a verb or adjective

angle: the space between two lines that start from a common point

antonym: a word that has an opposite meaning to another word

area: the number of squares needed to cover a surface

C

compare: to tell or show similarities

congruent: geometric figures that have the same size and shape

contrast: to tell or show differences

coordinating conjunction: words that join words, phrases, and sentences

D

declarative sentence: a sentence that makes a statement

denominator: the number written below the line in a fraction; it refers to the number of equal parts

detail: tells more about the main idea

diameter: a chord that joins two points on a circle and passes through the center

E

equation: a number sentence that shows two values are equal

equivalent: having the same value or showing equalness

exclamatory sentence: a sentence that expresses strong feeling

F

fact: a statement that can be proven and that everyone accepts as true

fiction: stories written from the imagination; not true

fluency: the ability to recognize and read words quickly and accurately

formula: a statement of a mathematical rule using letters

H

homophone: words that sound the same but are spelled differently and have different meanings

horizontal line: a line with the direction of left to right

hyperbole: exaggerated figure of speech

I

idiom: a figure of speech that cannot be taken literally; used to describe situations or events

imperative sentence: a sentence that gives a command

interrogative sentence: a sentence that asks a question

M

main idea: the main topic, usually of a piece of writing, such as a paragraph

mixed number: a value represented by a whole number and a fraction

Glossary *(cont.)*

metaphor: a comparison of two things that does not use the words *like* or *as*

multiple meaning words: words that have more than one meaning

N

narrative: one type of writing that gives the details of an experience or event.

negative number: a number with a value of less than zero

nonfiction: true accounts of an object or event in book or story form

numerator: the number written above the line in a fraction; it refers to the number of equal parts being referenced

O

obtuse angle: an angle that measures more than 90 degrees

opinion: one person's idea; everyone does not have to accept that it is correct.

P

parallel: lines that do not intersect

perimeter: the measure around the outside of a particular space

perpendicular: intersecting lines that form four 90 degree angles

personification: to give human characteristics to objects

predicate: any part of a sentence that is not part of the subject (usually the verb, describing words, and clauses)

prime number: a number that is only divisible by one and itself

R

radius: a line segment with one point in the center of a circle and the other point on the circumference of the circle

right angle: an angle that measures 90 degrees

root word: a word before prefixes or suffixes have been added to it

rounding: a way of working with numbers to make estimates

S

simile: a comparison of two things using the words like or as

subject: a noun or pronoun that tells who or what a sentence is about

summary: a shorter statement of a larger work

synonym: words that have the same or almost the same meaning

T

thesaurus: a book with synonyms and antonyms for words

V

vertical line: a line with the direction of top to bottom or up and down

Glosario

A

adjetivo: palabra que describe a un sustantivo o pronombre

adverbio: palabra que describe a un verbo o adjetivo

ángulo: el espacio entre dos líneas que parten de un mismo punto

ángulo agudo: ángulo que mide menos de 90 grados

ángulo obtuso: ángulo que mide más de 90 grados

ángulo recto: ángulo que mide 90 grados

antónimo: palabra cuyo significado es opuesto al de otra palabra

área: cantidad de cuadrados que se necesitan para cubrir una superficie

C

comparar: indicar o mostrar similitudes

congruente: figuras geométricas que tienen la misma forma y tamaño

conjunción coordinante: palabras que unen palabras, frases y oraciones

contrastar: indicar o mostrar diferencias

D

denominador: número que se escribe debajo de la línea de fracción; se refiere a la cantidad de partes iguales en las que se divide la unidad

detalle: da más información sobre la idea principal

diámetro: línea que une dos puntos en un círculo y pasa por el centro

E

ecuación: oración numérica que muestra qué dos valores son iguales

equivalente: que tiene el mismo valor o muestra equidad

F

ficción: historias escritas desde la imaginación; no son reales

fluidez: la capacidad de reconocer y leer las palabras rápidamente y con precisión

fórmula: enunciado de una regla matemática que usa letras

H

hecho: afirmación que se puede comprobar y que todos aceptan como verdadera

hipérbole: forma de expresión exagerada

homófono: palabras que suenan igual pero se escriben distinto y tienen distinto significado

I

idea principal: tema principal de un texto, por ejemplo un párrafo

L

línea horizontal: línea en dirección de izquierda a derecha

línea vertical: línea que va de arriba a abajo

M

metáfora: comparación de dos cosas donde no se usa la palabra "como"

Glosario *(cont.)*

modismo: forma de expresión que no se puede tomar literalmente, que se usa para describir situaciones o eventos

narración: un tipo de redacción que da detalles sobre una experiencia o acontecimiento

no ficción: relato de un evento o descripción de un objeto real en un libro o en forma de historia

numerador: número que se escribe arriba de la línea de fracción; se refiere a la cantidad de partes iguales de la unidad

número mixto: valor representado por un número entero y una fracción

número negativo: número cuyo valor es menor que cero

número primo: número que sólo es divisible por uno y por sí mismo

opinión: lo que piensa una persona. No todos tienen que estar de acuerdo con ella.

oración enunciativa: oración que hace una declaración

oración exclamativa: oración que expresa un sentimiento fuerte

oración imperativa: oración que da una orden

oración interrogativa: oración que hace una pregunta

palabra raíz: una palabra antes de que se le agreguen prefijos o sufijos

palabras de varios significados: palabras que tienen más de un significado

paralelo: rectas que no se cruzan

perímetro: la medida alrededor del exterior de un espacio dado

perpendicular: rectas secantes que forman cuatro ángulos de 90 grados

personificación: dar características humanas a los objetos

predicado: cualquier parte de una oración que no sea parte del sujeto, por lo general el verbo, palabras descriptivas y proposiciones

radio: segmento de recta con un extremo en el centro de un círculo y el otro en la circunferencia del círculo

redondear: una manera de trabajar con números para hacer estimaciones

refrán: ver modismo

resumen: un enunciado más corto de un trabajo más largo

símil: comparación de dos cosas usando palabras como "como" o "igual que"

sinónimo: palabras que tienen el mismo o casi el mismo significado

sujeto: sustantivo o pronombre que indica sobre qué o quién es la oración

tesauro: libro con sinónimos y antónimos de las palabras

Tips for Using This Book

This book has been designed to provide your child practice with skills and concepts while your child is on break from school. The book is divided into six weekly units. Each week has 10 pages of language arts and math practice. At the end of each week there is a challenge project for which your child may have to use several skills and concepts. Following are some tips for using this book with your child.

- Set aside a specific time of day to work on the book. This will establish consistency. An alternative is to look for times in your day or week that are less hectic and more conducive to practicing skills.

- Emphasize completing a couple of pages each time your child works in the book, rather than an entire week's worth of activity pages at one time. Completing several pages each day helps your child continually review and practice.

- Keep all practice sessions with your child positive and constructive. If the mood becomes tense, or you and your child get frustrated, set the book aside and look for another time for your child to practice.

- Help with instructions, if necessary. If your child is having difficulty understanding what to do, work some of the problems through with him or her.

- An answer key is provided on pages 97–100 at the back of this book. Once your child has completed the desired number of pages for the day, help your child check his or her work. If possible, take time to go back and correct any problems missed. Help your child learn from his or her mistakes.

- A completion certificate is provided at the end of each week. Once your child has completed the pages for a week, complete the certificate together. Filling out the certificate validates the importance of the work he or she has done, as well as shows a goal has been met.

Consejos para usar este libro

Este libro ha sido diseñado para que su hijo o hija practique destrezas y conceptos mientras está de vacaciones de la escuela. El libro está dividido en seis unidades semanales. Cada semana tiene 10 páginas para practicar artes del lenguaje y matemáticas. Al final de cada semana, hay un proyecto de desafío en el que su hijo puede usar diversas destrezas y conceptos. A continuación ofrecemos algunos consejos para usar este libro junto con su hijo.

- Dedique una hora del día en especial para trabajar con el libro. De esta forma establecerá regularidad. Una alternativa es buscar momentos del día o la semana que sean menos ajetreados y más propicios para practicar las destrezas.

- Insista en completar un par de páginas cada vez que su hijo trabaje en el libro en lugar de hacer al mismo tiempo las actividades para toda la semana. Completar varias páginas por día ayudará a su hijo a repasar y practicar continuamente.

- Haga que las sesiones de práctica con su hijo sean positivas y constructivas. Si el estado de ánimo se pone tenso, o si usted o su hijo se sienten frustrados, deje el libro y busque otro momento para que su hijo practique.

- Ayúdelo con las instrucciones si es necesario. Si su hijo tiene problemas para entender lo que debe hacer, trabaje con él en algunos de los problemas.

- En las páginas 97 a 100 del libro están las respuestas. Cuando su hijo haya completado la cantidad de páginas deseada para ese día, ayúdelo a corregir su trabajo. Si es posible, dedique un momento a volver atrás y corregir los problemas en que se equivocó. Ayude a su hijo a aprender de sus errores.

- Al final de cada semana se proporciona un certificado de terminación. Cuando su hijo haya completado las páginas de la semana, llenen el certificado juntos. Llenar el certificado da validez a la importancia del trabajo realizado y además muestra que se ha cumplido un objetivo.

Weekly Activities for Students

Actividades semanales para estudiantes

Reading Comprehension

Read the passages in the boxes below and answer the questions.

Lee cada texto y luego responde a las preguntas a continuación.

> Diane loves the animals at the zoo. She has been going to the zoo since she was a little girl. Her father works at the zoo. He takes pictures of the animals for the zoo newspaper. Diane helps her father set up his cameras and lights. Most of the time he takes still shots. He has to wait until the animals are in the right pose. Then he snaps the picture. Sometimes he takes moving pictures. Diane thinks he has the best job. She thinks he has the best job in the world.

1. Which of these would go best after the last sentence?
    A. Her father likes taking pictures of the monkeys best.
    B. Sometimes her father takes pictures of the fish in the aquariums.
    C. Someday she hopes to have a job taking pictures at the zoo, too.
    D. Our fourth grade class took a trip to the zoo this fall.

2. How can you best combine the last two sentences?
    J. The best job in the world is what Diane thinks her father has.
    K. Diane thinks her father has the best job in the world.
    L. Diane thinks this is the best job in the world and her father has it.
    M. Diane thinks her father has the best job. The best job in the world.

3. Which of these sentences does not belong in this paragraph?
    A. Some of the animals seem to like having their pictures taken.
    B. In the spring they will come and take pictures of our fourth grade class.
    C. It is hard for Diane's father to get pictures of the animals that only come out at night.
    D. Diane is learning a lot about taking pictures of animals from her father.

4. What is the main reason this paragraph was written?
    J. to tell how to take good pictures of zoo animals
    K. to tell about the different animals a girl sees at the zoo
    L. to tell about a girl who helps her father take pictures of animals at the zoo
    M. to tell about animals at the zoo that like their pictures taken

Imagine one of the pictures Diane's father might take. Write several sentences that describe the scene. If you wish, you may draw what you imagine on another sheet of paper.

_____

_____

_____

_____

_____

Comprehension Review: Stated Details

Read the paragraph. Use the information in the paragraph to complete the sentences. Circle your answers below.

Lee el párrafo. Contesta las preguntas usando le información en el párrafo. Encierra en un círculo tus respuestas.

Sir Walter Raleigh was an English explorer, soldier, and writer in the later 1500s and early 1600s. He was also a good friend of Queen Elizabeth I of England. According to one story, Raleigh was once visiting the queen at her court. They were out walking. When they reached a large puddle, the queen stopped. Ever the gentleman, Raleigh took off his coat. He spread it on the ground, so the queen could walk on it. He didn't want the queen to get her feet or clothes wet. No one knows if this story is true. We do know that Raleigh and the queen were friends. She made him a knight in 1585. She gave him a large piece of land in Ireland. He, in turn, helped the English defeat the Spanish at sea in 1588. He also sent colonists to North America in the 1580s. The two colonies founded on Roanoke Island did not succeed.

Fluency Goal: Read 120 words in one minute. The highlighted word is the 120th word in the passage. See pages 12 and 13 for information on fluency.

Meta para la fluidez: Leer 120 palabras en un minuto. La palabra destacada es la palabra número 120 en la historia. Ver las páginas 12 y 13 para más información sobre la fluidez de la lectura.

1. Sir Walter Raleigh was a friend of Queen _____.
   A. Mary   **B.** Elizabeth I   **C.** Anne   **D.** Elaine

2. In _____, the queen made Raleigh a knight.
   A. 1580   **B.** 1585   **C.** 1588   **D.** 1590

3. According to one story, Raleigh took off his coat so that _____.
   A. the queen could walk on it   **C.** he wouldn't be hot
   B. he could use it as a pillow   **D.** the queen could wear it

4. Raleigh did not succeed in setting up colonies in _____.
   A. England   **B.** Spain   **C.** North America   **D.** Ireland

5. The queen gave Raleigh a large piece of land in _____.
   A. England   **B.** Spain   **C.** North America   **D.** Ireland

6. What word does not describe Sir Walter Raleigh?
   A. friendly   **B.** thoughtful   **C.** landless   **D.** adventurous

Main Idea Story Parts

Read each story and then write a sentence that best tells the main idea.

Lee cada historia y luego escribe una oración que exprese la idea principal.

The students in Mrs. Lee's class were having a great time at the Riverside Zoo. As they were walking to visit the chimpanzees again, Mrs. Lee suddenly stopped. "Is anyone wearing a watch?" she asked. "I'm afraid that mine has stopped."

Amanda looked at her watch. "It's 1:40," she said.

Mrs. Lee's eyes opened wide. "Oh, no! We were supposed to meet Mrs. Miles's class at 1:30. We're late!"

Mrs. Lee and her students began running for the bus.

Main idea: _____

_____

One of the penguins was ready to play. He waddled up the icy hill as fast as he could. Then he flopped onto his stomach and slid down. Some of the penguins were eating lunch. They swallowed the fish as quickly as the zookeeper could empty the big buckets of food. A few of the penguins were sleeping quietly.

The children watched the penguins for a long time. When it was time to leave the exhibit, all of the children were sad to go. Many of the children liked the penguins exhibit best.

Main idea: _____

_____

Addition and Subtraction Word Problems

Solve the following problems. Circle the important facts you need to solve them. Use the space provided for scratch work.

Soluciona los siguientes problemas. Encierra en un círculo los datos importantes que necesites y resuélvelo. Usa el espacio provisto para encontrar la solución a cada problema.

---

1. There were 76 students in a school jog-a-thon. Twenty-six of them were in 3rd grade, 28 of them were in 4th grade, and 22 of them were in 5th grade.

   a. How many 4th- and 5th-grade students were in the jog-a-thon?

   _____

   b. Which grade had the most students in the jog-a-thon? _____

2. The jog-a-thon route covered 150 kilometers. There were 4 rest stops for the runners. Niki ran 52 kilometers and stopped at the second rest stop.

   a. How much further does Niki have to run to complete the route? _____

   b. Had she gone at least half the distance? _____

---

3. Melita's team wanted to collect a total of $325.00. They collected $208.75 from the jog-a-thon and $76.20 from a candy sale.

   a. How much money did they collect? _____

   b. Would they collect more money from 3 candy sales than from 1 jog-a-thon? _____

4. Twenty team members had lunch together at the third rest stop. They had traveled 70 kilometers. Thirteen team members drank milk with their lunch and the rest drank grape juice.

   a. How many team members drank grape juice? _____

   b. How many students did not drink grape juice? _____

---

5. Bill, Holly, and Katie collected contributions from their neighbors. Bill collected $13.78, Holly collected $16.85, and Katie collected $12.34.

   a. How much more did Holly collect than Bill? _____

   b. How much did Holly and Katie collect together? _____

6. To get ready, Carol bought new shoes for $36.00 and a new water bottle for $1.36. Her mom gave her $47.00 to spend.

   a. How much did she spend for the shoes and water bottle? _____

   b. How much more were the shoes than the water bottle? _____

Define It

Each of these words has more than one meaning.

Cada una de estas palabras tiene más de un significado.

1. **wind**
   a. a movement of the air
   b. to twist around

2. **close**
   a. to bring parts of edges together (*close* a book)
   b. not far apart

3. **record**
   a. to put sound or pictures onto something that can be listened to or watched later
   b. the best in achievement in a category (set a *record* in a sport)

4. **part**
   a. one of the sections something is divided into
   b. to leave someone; go away (*part* from a friend)

5. **conduct**
   a. to lead (*conduct* the band)
   b. personal behavior (*conduct* oneself well at school)

Choose one meaning for each word. Write the letter of the definition you chose in the blank before each word. Then write the word in a sentence that shows the meaning.

Elige un significado para cada palabra. Escribe la letra de la definición en el espacio en blanco que está antes de cada palabra. Después, escribe la palabra en una oración que muestre su significado.

_____ 1. **wind** _____

_____

_____ 2. **close** _____

_____

_____ 3. **record** _____

_____

_____ 4. **part** _____

_____

_____ 5. **conduct** _____

_____

Complete the Sentences

Sentences begin with capital letters and end with a period, exclamation point, or question mark. Every sentence must also have a subject and a predicate. Here are some incomplete sentences. Complete them, being sure to add punctuation at the end.

Las oraciones empiezan con mayúsculas y terminan con un punto, signo de exclamación o signo de interrogación. Cada oración debe incluir un sujeto y un predicado. Aquí hay algunas oraciones incompletas. Complétalas, asegúrate de agregar la puntuación al final.

1. Sandy cried when she _____

_____

2. The best place in the world to _____

_____

3. Who can _____

_____

4. I wish I had _____

_____

5. There aren't many _____

_____

6. This is the best_____

_____

7. It's times like this that _____

_____

8. When are you going to_____

_____

9. I can't believe _____

_____

10. It was the _____

_____

Subtraction Solutions

Fill in the puzzle by solving the subtraction problems and writing the words for their answers in the puzzle.

Completa el acertijo resolviendo los problemas de sustracción y escribe las palabras de la respuesta en el acertijo.

Across

1. 25 – 11 =
3. 40 – 21 =
7. 33 – 16 =
9. 51 – 35 =

Down

1. 46 – 31 =
2. 27 – 7 =
4. 22 – 4 =
5. 19 – 8 =
6. 44 – 32 =
8. 38 – 25 =

Take Your Pick

Look at the lists of subjects and predicates. Choose any five subjects and predicates and write five sentences. Add to the sentences to make them more interesting. Remember to use a capital letter at the beginning of each sentence and punctuation at the end.

Observa las listas de sujetos y predicados. Elige cinco sujetos y predicados cualquiera y escribe cinco oraciones. Recuerda empezar cada oración con mayúscula y terminar con la puntuación correcta.

Example: The giant oak tree swayed lazily in the warm breeze.

Ejemplo: El roble gigante se meneaba ligeramente en la brisa cálida.

Subjects	Predicates
a horse	jumped on a lily pad
a bullfrog	baked a birthday cake
I	walked down my street
my mother	wrote a letter
my friend	crashed the car
a giant	danced a jig
that snake	sang a song
my sister	jumped off the bridge
the clown	landed on my head
the parrot	skipped backwards
the monkey	played the piano
the teacher	blindfolded me
an organ grinder	skipped and whistled

1. _____

2. _____

3. _____

4. _____

5. _____

Secret Message

Add or subtract. Write the letter that goes with each answer on the line to reveal a secret message.

Suma o resta. Escribe la letra que le corresponde a cada respuesta en la línea para revelar un mensaje secreto.

1. 810,842 890,013 + 105,831 = O	**2.** 964,116 − 106,115 = A	**3.** 260,303 − 173,992 = Y	**4.** 472,574 299,748 + 616,325 = C
5. 204,582 − 170,425 = R	**6.** 580,590 131,226 + 890,304 = S	**7.** 935,365 461,342 + 915,762 = N	**8.** 875,718 − 469,958 = U
9. 500,581 − 487,643 = L	**10.** 169,748 171,071 + 167,011 = !	**11.** 237,114 − 193,357 = T	

_____ _____ _____   _____ _____
1,602,120 858,001 86,311   2,312,469 1,806,686

___ ___   ___ ___ ___ ___ ___ ___ ___ ___ ___ ___ ___ ___
43,757 1,806,686   1,388,647 858,001 12,938 1,388,647 405,760 12,938 858,001 43,757 1,806,686 34,157 1,602,120 507,830

Sign In

Place + and – signs between the digits so that both sides of each equation are equal.

Coloca signos + y – entre los dígitos para que ambos lados de cada ecuación sean iguales.

1.	6 4 1 2 6 2 = 15
2.	9 1 3 1 4 1 = 5
3.	9 3 4 1 2 3 = 14
4.	5 1 1 3 4 6 = 18
5.	9 8 6 3 5 3 = 8
6.	2 1 8 9 3 5 = 20
7.	5 3 2 4 1 5 = 12
8.	4 9 3 7 3 1 = 11
9.	7 6 2 8 7 1 = 3
10.	9 9 9 2 2 8 = 1

Challenge Project for Week 1

Choose nonfiction material to read. Remember, nonfiction is about something real. You can find such material in a book, a newspaper, or a magazine. It can be about a real person, place, animal, or thing. After you have read it, complete the form below.

Elige material de no ficción para leer. Recuerda, la no ficción trata de algo real. Puedes encontrar este tipo de material en un libro, periódico o revista. Puede ser sobre una persona, lugar, animal o cosa real. Después de leerlo, completa la forma siguiente.

Nonfiction Reading Journal

Topic: _____

Source: _____

Pages: _____

Note: Use another piece of paper if you wish.

I chose this topic because _____

I know the following facts about this topic:

1. _____

2. _____

3. _____

4. _____

I have the following questions about this topic:

1. _____

2. _____

3. _____

I learned the following new facts about this topic:

1. _____

2. _____

3. _____

4. _____

I would like to learn more about:

_____

_____

_____

Fantastic News!

This is to report that _____

(Name)

has successfully completed all the activity pages for week 1.

Congratulations!

_____

(Date)

Main Idea of a Paragraph

It is easy to write the main idea of a paragraph. Read the paragraph carefully and answer the three Ws (who, what, and why). You do not need to use complete sentences here. Then make a good sentence out of your answers. Read your new sentence carefully to make sure it makes sense. Practice with the paragraph below.

Es fácil escribir la idea principal de un párrafo. Lee el párrafo con atención y responde las tres W (who, what y why). No tienes que usar oraciones completas aquí. Después, crea una oración correcta con tus respuestas. Lee la nueva oración atentamente para asegurarte de que tiene sentido. Practica con el párrafo siguiente.

Lola loved to watch the big, beautiful birds from South America. She stared at the parrots' bright green wings as the birds flew gracefully in their giant bird cage. Lola laughed when they called to each other with loud, squeaky voices. The parrots were Lola's favorite animals at the zoo.

1. Who? _____

2. What? _____

3 Why? _____

4. Write a sentence that tells the main idea using your answers.

_____

_____

Check to make sure your sentence is complete.
Verifica para que te asegures que tu oración esté completa.

1. Does your sentence make sense? ☐

2. Does it start with a capital letter? ☐

3. Does it end with a period? ☐

Adjectives and Adverbs

Adjectives are used to modify nouns and pronouns. Adverbs are used to modify verbs, adjectives, and other adverbs. Both are used to make writing more specific and interesting.

Los Adjetivos son usados para modificar a los pronombres. Los adverbios son usados para modificar a los verbos, adjetivos y otros adverbios. Ambos son usados para hacer la escritura más específica e interesante.

➤ **Add adjectives and adverbs to the following sentences to make them more specific and interesting.**

➤ **Agrega adjetivos y adverbios a las siguentes oraciones para que sean más interesantes.**

example: The car ran into the truck.

The red, shiny Mustang convertible suddenly ran into the four-door, white Dodge pickup.

1. The dog barked at the cat.

   _____

   _____

2. The clown entertained the crowd.

   _____

   _____

3. I hit the ball.

   _____

   _____

4. Mei Ling ate lunch.

   _____

   _____

5. Everyone watched Rafael play basketball.

   _____

   _____

6. Johnny gave Mustafa toys.

   _____

   _____

7. Cows marched through the meadow.

   _____

   _____

Multiplication Practice

Complete the multiplication problems. The first one is done for you as an example.

Completa los problemas de multiplicación. El primero ya ha sido resuelto para usar como ejemplo.

1.
```
     1
     1
    53
  x 54
   212
+ 2,650
  2,862
```

2.
```
   25
 x 36
```

3.
```
   36
 x 72
```

4.
```
   49
 x 23
```

5.
```
   54
 x 23
```

6.
```
   76
 x 53
```

7.
```
   67
 x 29
```

8.
```
   45
 x 78
```

9.
```
   92
 x 14
```

10.
```
   87
 x 72
```

11.
```
   19
 x 91
```

12.
```
   54
 x 54
```

13.
```
   98
 x 89
```

14.
```
   34
 x 43
```

15.
```
   75
 x 57
```

16.
```
   52
 x 25
```

17. 23 x 56 = _____

18. 67 x 78 = _____

Frontier Words

Frontier living generated many new words that were commonly used by the pioneers. Figure out these words by reading the clues first. Then find the coordinates on the grid below.

Write the letter that is in that space on the proper lines. (To find the coordinates, go across the first number of spaces. From there, count up the second number of spaces.)

La vida en la frontera generó muchas palabras nuevas que eran comúnmente usadas por los pioneros. Encuentra estas palabras leyendo las pistas primero. Después encuentra las coordenadas en el cuadro siguiente.

Escribe la letra que está en ese espacio en la línea apropiada. (Para encontrar las coordenadas, cuenta hacia la derecha el primer número. De ahí, cuenta hacia arriba el segundo número.)

4	l	d	s	i	g	e	m	c	p	s	u	g	l	a	t
3	f	e	a	n	r	o	i	u	i	h	e	u	o	n	d
2	p	o	h	e	m	a	s	f	c	y	m	t	p	r	s
1	c	a	e	y	l	t	g	r	o	n	d	o	a	f	s
0	1	2	3	4	5	6	7	8	9	10	11	12	13	14	15

1. ___ ___ ___ ___ ___ is a prairie sod house.
   3,4 13,3 2,4 11,1 10,2

2. ___ ___ ___ ___   ___ ___ ___ ___ ___ ___ ___ are also known as johnnycakes.
   8,4 9,1 5,3 4,3   15,3 2,2 2,4 5,4 6,4 14,2 7,2

3. ___ ___ ___ ___ ___ - ___ ___ ___ ___ ___ ___ rushed to California to find gold.
   8,2 12,1 8,1 15,4 4,1   4,3 7,3 10,1 3,1 5,3 10,4

4. ___ ___ ___ ___ ___ are dried buffalo manure used for fires.
   8,4 3,2 9,3 13,2 3,4

5. ___ ___ ___ ___ ___ ___ ___ ___ ___ are settlers of the western frontier.
   4,2 7,4 4,4 7,1 5,3 2,1 14,3 6,1 7,2

6. ___ ___ ___ ___ is a disease now known as malaria.
   6,2 12,4 8,3 11,3

7. ___ ___ ___ ___ ___ ___ ___ ___ are thieves who stole cattle.
   5,3 11,4 15,2 6,1 13,4 2,3 8,1 15,1

8. Prairie ___ ___ ___ ___ ___ ___ ___ ___ is a nickname for a covered wagon.
   7,2 1,1 10,3 2,2 9,1 14,3 3,1 5,3

Sentence Emergencies

These sentences need your help. Be a sentence doctor and make these sentences better.
Rewrite the sentences correctly. Use capital letters and punctuation correctly.

Estas oraciones necesitan tu ayuda. Juega al médico de oraciones y ayúdalas a mejorar. Vuelve a escribir las oraciones correctamente. Coloca una mayúscula al comienzo de cada oración. Usa un punto, un signo de interrogación o un signo de exclamación al final de cada oración.

1. yes we go to the library on tuesday

   _____

2. mrs smith is your teacher

   _____

3. the students in mr garcias class were reading charlottes web

   _____

4. what a wonderful day it is

   _____

5. jordan, come play with us in griffith park

   _____

6. watch out, michelle

   _____

7. maria what is your favorite kind of math problem

   _____

8. i will paint johns room today

   _____

9. what time is the lunch at sunset diner

   _____

10. i got a sticker a book and a magazine at waldens drug store

    _____

Practice Multiplication and Division

Fill in the missing factors.

Completa los factores que faltan.

1. $9 \times \underline{\hspace{1cm}} = 54$

2. $3 \times \underline{\hspace{1cm}} = 36$

3. $10 \times \underline{\hspace{1cm}} = 60$

4. $8 \times \underline{\hspace{1cm}} = 64$

5. $\underline{\hspace{1cm}} \times 9 = 81$

6. $6 \times \underline{\hspace{1cm}} = 72$

7. $9 \times \underline{\hspace{1cm}} = 45$

8. $4 \times \underline{\hspace{1cm}} = 48$

9. $\underline{\hspace{1cm}} \times 7 = 42$

10. $\underline{\hspace{1cm}} \times 7 = 63$

11. $\underline{\hspace{1cm}} \times 9 = 63$

12. $5 \times \underline{\hspace{1cm}} = 55$

13. $6 \times \underline{\hspace{1cm}} = 36$

14. $\underline{\hspace{1cm}} \times 4 = 36$

15. $\underline{\hspace{1cm}} \times 6 = 54$

16. $\underline{\hspace{1cm}} \times 9 = 99$

17. $7 \times \underline{\hspace{1cm}} = 49$

18. $9 \times \underline{\hspace{1cm}} = 63$

19. $42 \div 7 = \underline{\hspace{1cm}}$

20. $54 \div 9 = \underline{\hspace{1cm}}$

21. $54 \div 6 = \underline{\hspace{1cm}}$

22. $12 \div 3 = \underline{\hspace{1cm}}$

23. $88 \div 8 = \underline{\hspace{1cm}}$

24. $48 \div 12 = \underline{\hspace{1cm}}$

25. $56 \div 7 = \underline{\hspace{1cm}}$

26. $56 \div 8 = \underline{\hspace{1cm}}$

27. $96 \div 8 = \underline{\hspace{1cm}}$

28. $18 \div \underline{\hspace{1cm}} = 6$

29. $44 \div \underline{\hspace{1cm}} = 4$

30. $72 \div \underline{\hspace{1cm}} = 8$

31. $33 \div \underline{\hspace{1cm}} = 3$

32. $120 \div \underline{\hspace{1cm}} = 10$

33. $77 \div \underline{\hspace{1cm}} = 11$

34. $24 \div \underline{\hspace{1cm}} = 4$

35. $49 \div \underline{\hspace{1cm}} = 7$

36. $16 \div \underline{\hspace{1cm}} = 2$

Put Them in Order

Read the sentences. Then, rewrite them in a paragraph in the correct sequence. Write another paragraph to continue the story.

Lee las oraciones. Vuelve a escribirlas en un párrafo en el orden correcto. Escribe otro párrafo para continuar la historia.

I got out of bed and looked in the mirror.
I ran to my mother to show her what had happened.
She said, "It appears that those seeds you swallowed yesterday have been planted inside you."
I woke up one morning feeling strange.
Then she looked in the phone book for a good gardener to come over to trim me.
What a shock I got when I saw a plant growing out of my ears!
I am feeling better now, but I still have to water myself every day.

_____

_____

_____

_____

_____

_____

_____

_____

Circus Balloon

Finish the story below. Use good descriptive words in your story.

Termina la historia siguiente. Usa palabras descriptivas en tu historia.

A man from the circus filled the boy's large, red balloon with helium and tied it to a long, white string. The boy held the string tightly in his hand and walked over to see the enormous, gray elephant. All of a sudden, a brisk wind . . .

_____

_____

_____

_____

_____

_____

_____

_____

_____

_____

_____

_____

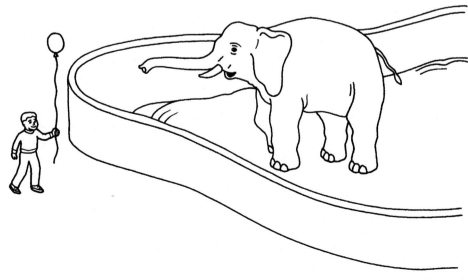

Practice Calculating Areas

- To compute the area of a rectangle, multiply the length times the width.
- Area = length x width
- A = *l* x w

- *Para obtener el área de un rectángulo, multiplica lo largo por lo ancho.*
- *Area = largo x ancho*
- *A = l x a*

6 cm

4 cm

A = 6 x 4

A = 24 square centimeters = 24 sq. cm

Compute the area of each rectangle.

Calcula el área de cada rectángulo.

1.   3 cm

5 cm

A = _____

2.   9 cm

6 cm

A = _____

3.   7 in.

8 in.

A = _____

4.   10 in.

7 in.

A = _____

5.   20 in.

9 in.

A = _____

6.   18 in.

7 in.

A = _____

7.   9 mm

11 mm

A = _____

8.   25 mm

9 mm

A = _____

9.   12 cm

8 cm

A = _____

Thesaurus Practice

Here is an entry from a thesaurus. Use it to answer the questions.

Aquí está una entrada de un tesauro. Úsala para contestar las preguntas.

> **anger:** 1. *n.* wrath, rage, fury, temper
> *Ant.* patience, mildness, calm
> 2. *v.* infuriate, annoy, irritate

1. **You can tell from this thesaurus entry that someone who is <u>angry</u> is**
   - **A.** not happy
   - **B.** feeling good
   - **C.** very calm
   - **D.** ready to eat

Read this sentence.

Lee esta oración.

> It is important to control how you show your anger.

2. **Which *synonym* could be used to replace the word <u>anger</u> in the sentence?**
   - **A.** patience
   - **B.** temper
   - **C.** annoy
   - **D.** calmness

Read this sentence.

Lee esta oración.

> My little sister annoys me when she gives me a hug.

3. **Which *antonym* could be used to replace the word <u>annoys</u> in the sentence?**
   - **A.** calms
   - **B.** infuriates
   - **C.** irritates
   - **D.** tickles

Challenge Project for Week 2

Use the format below to write your own newspaper article about an event in your neighborhood.

Usa el formato siguiente para escribir tu propio artículo de periódico sobre algún evento en tu vecindario.

The Neighborhood News

Week of_____

Feature of the Week

_____

_____

_____

_____

_____

_____

Picture of the Week

_____

_____

_____

_____

_____

_____

_____

_____

_____

_____

Way To Go!

_____
(Name)

You did a great job on the activity pages for week 2.

_____
(Date)

Synonym and Antonym Review

Synonyms are words that have the same or almost the same meanings.
Antonyms are words that have the opposite meanings.

Los sinónimos son palabras que tienen el mismo o casi el mismo significado.
Los antónimos son palabras que tienen significados opuestos.

Read the words below. Write **S** next to the synonyms and **A** next to the antonyms.

Lee las siguientes palabras. Escribe una **S** junto a los sinónimos y una **A** junto a los antónimos.

1. heat, warmth	S	11. quiet, loud	
2. litter, trash		12. buy, sell	
3. happy, sad		13. angry, mad	
4. speak, talk		14. bright, shiny	
5. hot, cold		15. long, short	
6. hard, soft		16. dark, light	
7. fast, slow		17. mild, gentle	
8. wet, damp		18. loss, gain	
9. loud, noisy		19. remember, forget	
10. hungry, starving		20. ignore, disregard	

Specific Details

Cross out the sentences that do not support the topic sentence of this paragraph. Then, rewrite the edited paragraph on the lines below.

En los renglones siguientes, tacha las oraciones que no respaldan la oración temática de este párrafo. Entonces reescribe el párrafo editado en las siguientes lineas.

Camping Is Fun

Camping is fun for many reasons. It is fun to be out in the country, far away from the cares of everyday life. I don't have to worry about things like chores and homework. I got a good grade on my last homework assignment, though. Even though there are camping chores I must do, somehow they are duties I look forward to. Last week at school I had hall duty. I enjoy building a campfire and keeping it going. Our home fireplace uses gas. If we are camping near a lake or stream, I can go fishing, one of my favorite pastimes. I can't remember whether I put plenty of food in my fish tank at home. There is nothing better than freshly caught fish cooked over an open campfire. My mother says that the fish at our local market do not always seem fresh to her. Yes, give me a camp in the woods, a roaring campfire, and fish to catch and eat, and I am truly a happy camper.

Fluency Goal: Read 120 words in one minute. The highlighted word is the 120th word in the passage. See pages 12 and 13 for information on fluency.

Meta para la fluidez: *Leer 120 palabras en un minuto. La palabra destacada es la palabra número 120 en la historia. Ver las páginas 12 y 13 para más información sobre la fluidez de la*

_____

_____

_____

_____

_____

_____

_____

_____

_____

Equation Practice

Fill in the box with the number that makes each number sentence true.

Completa el cuadro con el número que hace que cada oración numérica sea verdadera.

1. $6 + 5 = \boxed{} + 4$

2. $9 + 3 = 7 + \boxed{}$

3. $9 - 3 = 4 + \boxed{}$

4. $\boxed{} + 5 = 9 + 2$

5. $14 - 8 = \boxed{} + 6$

6. $7 + 13 = \boxed{} + 11$

7. $11 + 5 = \boxed{} + 6$

8. $5 + 3 = 4 + \boxed{}$

9. $10 + 9 = 5 + \boxed{}$

10. $\boxed{} + 6 = 10 - 2$

11. $13 + 8 = \boxed{} + 7$

12. $9 + 20 = \boxed{} + 10$

13. $14 - 9 = \boxed{} + 3$

14. $12 + 3 = 7 + \boxed{}$

15. $15 + 5 = 10 + \boxed{}$

16. $\boxed{} + 20 = 30 - 6$

17. $23 + 12 = \boxed{} + 15$

18. $12 + 12 = \boxed{} + 14$

19. $12 + 8 = \boxed{} + 10$

20. $13 + 12 = \boxed{} + 15$

21. $15 - 10 = \boxed{} + 2$

22. $10 + 3 = 7 + \boxed{}$

23. $25 + 5 = 15 + \boxed{}$

24. $\boxed{} + 11 = 22 + 9$

25. $9 + 11 = \boxed{} + 12$

26. $16 - 11 = \boxed{} + 3$

Tune In to Homophones

Homophones are words that sound alike but are spelled differently and have different meanings. Written on each television screen is a message. The messages are full of misused homophones. Rewrite the messages correcting the homophones.

Los homófonos son palabras que suenan igual pero que se escriben diferente y tienen significados diferentes. En cada pantalla de televisión hay un mensaje escrito. Los mensajes están llenos de homófonos mal usados. Vuelve a escribir los mensajes y corrige los homófonos.

1.

Whether Flash...heavy reigns dew inn an our.

_____

4.

Watch Mussel Man weakly lift waits on channel too.

_____

2.

Next on The Whirled Turns...Elizabeth is never scene again.

_____

5.

Special Announcement! Ice skating pear wins gold metals!

_____

3.

News Extra! A wild hoarse and dear escape from the zoo.

6.

Try a knew serial just for kids! Awesome Oats!

Writing by Sense

One of the best ways to write descriptively is to use your senses. Think about how something looks, smells, sounds, tastes, and feels, and then write about it, keeping those senses in mind. For example, instead of writing, "The puppies are cute," write, "The playful puppies roll over each other and tumble into a ball of fur and pink noses." This gives an idea of exactly how the puppies look. Sentences that use the senses to describe are much more interesting to read, and they make the images seem real for the reader.

Una de las mejores maneras para escribir descriptivamente es usar tus sentidos. Piensa en cómo algo se ve, huele, suena, sabe y se siente y después escribe sobre ello manteniendo lo que sientes en mente. Por ejemplo, en vez de escribir, "Los cachorros son lindos," escribe, "Los cachorros juguetones ruedan unos sobre otros y se enredan en una bola de pelaje y narices rosas." Esto da la idea exacta de cómo son los cachorros. Las oraciones que usan los sentidos para describir son mucho más interesantes para leer, y hacen que las imágenes parezcan reales para el lector.

Follow each direction below to write a sentence using one of the five senses.

Sigue las siguientes instrucciones y escribe una oración usando uno de los cinco sentidos.

1. Describe how a skyscraper **looks**. _____

_____

_____

2. Describe how a freshly mowed lawn **smells**. _____

_____

_____

3. Describe how a yipping dog **sounds**. _____

_____

_____

4. Describe how a lemon **tastes**. _____

_____

_____

5. Describe how a kitten **feels**. _____

_____

_____

Decimal Practice

Ordering Decimals

Write the decimals in order from smallest to largest.

Escribe los decimales en orden del más pequeño al más grande.

1. 0.39, 0.56, 0.75, 0.31 _____, _____, _____, _____

2. 0.59, 0.35, 0.67, 0.37 _____, _____, _____, _____

3. 1.12, 4.78, 6.74, 1.70 _____, _____, _____, _____

4. 10.04, 90.22, 62.34, 35.69 _____, _____, _____, _____

Whistle Stop Train Tours
Train Stops

Newtonville	4.22 miles	North Shore	37.16 miles
Crunch Town	20.07 miles	Dudley Town	27.70 miles
Red River Valley	26.96 miles	St. Barney	35.33 miles
Oakland Hills	10.88 miles	Grovertown	10.19 miles
Raisin City	20.10 miles	Restful Valley	8.18 miles

Write the towns in order from closest to farthest.

Escribe los pueblos en orden del más cercano al más lejano.

5. Restful Valley, Raisin City, North Shore

_____, _____, _____

6. Oakland Hills, Dudley Town, Crunch Town

_____, _____, _____

7. North Shore, St. Barney, Grovertown

_____, _____, _____

8. Red River Valley, Dudley Town, North Shore

_____, _____, _____

9. Restful Valley, Oakland Hills, St. Barney

_____, _____, _____

10. Newtonville, St. Barney, Raisin City

_____, _____, _____

Idioms

Idioms are expressions whose meanings are different from the literal ones. Explain what the idioms below actually mean.

Los modismos son expresiones cuyo significado es distinto del literal. Explica el verdadero significado de los siguientes modismos.

1. When Angelica said, "That movie **took my breath away**," she meant _____

   _____

2. "When Dad finally **put his foot down**, my brother started to do better in school," said

   Boris. What Boris meant was _____

   _____

3. Dana stood and said, "I guess I'll **hit the road** now." What Dana meant was

   _____

4. When Mario said that he was a bit **under the weather** last weekend, he meant that

   _____

5. When Nicholas said that he **slept like a log** last night, he meant _____

   _____

6. "I'll be **in the doghouse** for sure," exclaimed Roberto. What Roberto really meant was

   _____

7. "**Hold your horses**," remarked the police officer. The police officer meant _____

   _____

8. When Ryan asked Patricia, "Are you **getting cold feet**?" he was actually asking

   _____

9. If Grandpa loves **to spin a yarn**, he _____

   _____

10. When Leslie says that she is **in the dark** about what's going on, she means

   _____

Do You Speak Math?

Math or mathematics has a language all its own. To do math well in school, you need to understand this special language. Look at the words in Column 1. On the line provided, put the letter of its matching definition from Column 2.

Las matemáticas tienen su propio idioma. Para que te vaya bien en matemáticas en la escuela, tienes que entender este idioma especial. Observa las palabras de la Columna 1. En la línea provista, coloca la letra de la definición que le corresponde de la Columna 2.

Column 1

_____ 1. area

_____ 2. congruent

_____ 3. difference

_____ 4. equation

_____ 5. parallel

_____ 6. perimeter

_____ 7. perpendicular

_____ 8. product

_____ 9. quotient

_____ 10. sum

Column 2

A. a line that is at right angles to another line

B. the answer to a subtraction problem

C. lines that run side by side that never cross and never meet

D. the answer to an addition problem

E. equal in shape or size

F. the distance around the edge of a shape (side + side + side + side)

G. a number sentence or statement

H. the answer to a multiplication problem

I. the amount of surface within a given boundary. It is measured in square units.

J. the answer to a division problem

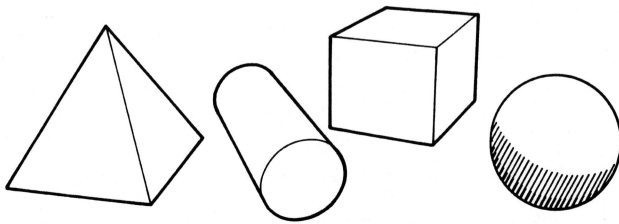

My Dog

Read the paragraph and answer the questions that follow it. Choose the correct answer.

Lee el párrafo y responde las preguntas a continuación. Completa los círculos junto a las respuestas correctas.

(1) Ricky, the dog who became my best friend, just mysteriously appeared at our house one day. (2) My mother said that his appearance was not really mysterious. (3) She thought that someone who no longer wanted him dropped him off near our house because that person knew we like dogs. (4) Because no one else in the family seemed much interested in him, I decided that Ricky was mine and that I would name him. (5) I named him Ricky because I was watching a singer I admired named Ricky on television when Dog Ricky appeared in our front yard. (6) Why anyone would not want to keep Ricky I could not understand, for he was a loving dog and a mild-mannered one if he did not think he was protecting me from villains. (7) It is true that I always felt safe when Ricky was around. (8) With him to protect me, I did not mind being home alone. (9) Also, I could always count on Ricky to be sympathetic if I thought someone had treated me unfairly or if I had suffered a disappointment of any kind. (10) His understanding eyes helped soothe my bruised heart every time. (11) Even when he became old and slow and his vision blurred, Ricky always came to my defense like a fierce tiger. (12) For my money, he had the best qualities a pet should have: Ricky was loyal and loving.

Fluency Goal: Read 120 words in one minute. The highlighted word is the 120th word in the passage. See pages 12 and 13 for information on fluency.

Meta para la fluidez: Leer 120 palabras en un minuto. La palabra destacada es la palabra número 120 en la historia. Ver las páginas 12 y 13 para más información sobre la fluidez de la lectura.

1. Which of these words is used as a transition?

   (a) I

   (b) Why

   (c) Also

   (d) Oh

   (e) none of these

2. Which is the topic sentence?

   (a) 12

   (b) 6

   (c) 5

   (d) 2

   (e) none of these

3. Which is the concluding sentence?

   (a) 1

   (b) 12

   (c) 10

   (d) 9

   (e) none of these

4. Which supporting details did the writer have in her paragraph?

   (a) appearance, name, safe, sympathy

   (b) mystery, name, old, barking

   (c) Mother, family, villains, money

   (d) Ricky, singer, safe, eyes, food

   (e) none of these

Order of Operations

Do the operation in (parentheses) first.

Haz el problema en (paréntesis) primero.

1. $(6 \times 3) \div 2$	2. $(3 \times 2) \div 6$	3. $(2 \times 6) \div 3$
4. $(8 \div 4) \times 2$	5. $(5 + 2) \times 4$	6. $(4 \div 2) \times 8$

Solve each word problem.

Resuelve cada problema escrito.

7. Lily had 10 jellybeans evenly distributed into 5 plastic sandwich bags. Her sister Billie had twice the number of jellybeans than in one of Lily's bags. How many jellybeans did Billie have in one bag?

   Billie had _____ jellybeans in one bag.

8. Grady had 10 jellybeans evenly distributed into 2 plastic sandwich bags. His brother Brady had 5 times the number of jellybeans than in one of Grady's bags. How many jellybeans did Brady have in one bag?

   Brady had _____ jellybeans in one bag.

Challenge Project for Week 3

Create a map of your neighborhood. Be as detailed as possible. Use symbols on your map and show what they represent in the map key.

Haz un mapa de tu vecindario. Usa la mayor cantidad posible de detalles. Usa símbolos en el mapa y muestra qué representan en la Clave del mapa.

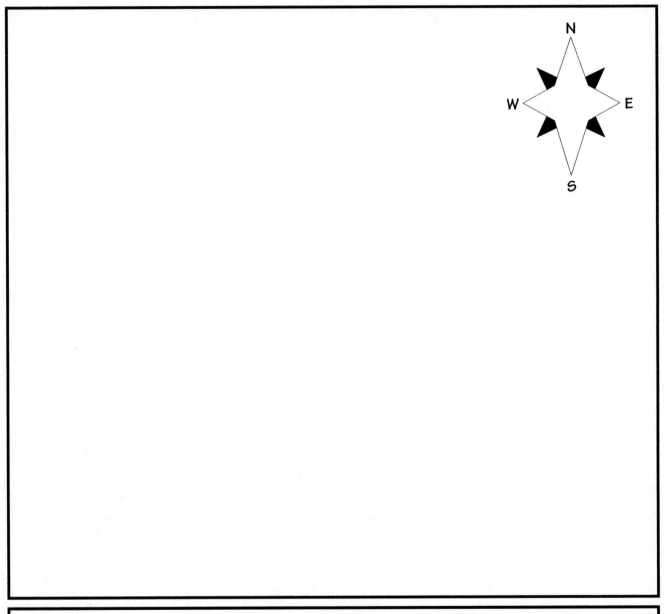

Map Key

Hooray!

GO TEAM

_____ (Name)

just finished all the activity pages for week 3.

_____ (Date)

Reading Comprehension

Read the story in the box below and answer the questions.

Lee el siguiente fragmento y luego responde las preguntas a continuación.

The Best Baker

Mrs. Swenson and Mr. Olson each put signs in the windows of their bakeries saying, "The Best Baker in the Land." Back and forth they argued, saying, "I am the best," "No, I am the best." The townspeople soon wearied of their constant bickering.

One day, the mayor announced that the king was coming to look for a new royal baker. "If one of you win," he told them, "it will be a great **honor**."

The two bakers baked for days to impress the king. When he arrived he looked over the cakes, cookies, and pies and cried, "But where is the bread?"

The two bakers looked at each other and said, "Bread?"

"You must bake bread for the King!" cried the Mayor.

"I have only a little flour and milk left," said Mrs. Swenson.

"I have only a little yeast and butter," said Mr. Olson.

"Fine. Then together you can bake bread," said the King.

Mr. Olson took his yeast and butter over to Mrs. Swenson's bakery. Mrs. Swenson put on her apron. Mr. Olson put on his hat. The bread was just finished when the Mayor ran in. "Hurry! The King is getting impatient." He grabbed the bread from the oven and raced down the street, with Mrs. Swenson and Mr. Olson behind him.

The King tasted the bread. He smiled. "This is the best bread I have ever tasted. You will both be royal bakers and bake my bread together."

Fluency Goal: Read 120 words in one minute. The highlighted word is the 120th word in the passage. See pages 12 and 13 for information on fluency.

Meta para la fluidez: *Leer 120 palabras en un minuto. La palabra destacada es la palabra número 120 en la historia. Ver las páginas 12 y 13 para más información sobre la fluidez de la lectura.*

1. Why were the bakers surprised when the king asked for bread?
   - **A.** They didn't know how to bake bread.
   - **B.** Kings do not eat bread.
   - **C.** They thought he wanted fancy pastries.
   - **D.** They had already baked bread.

2. This story takes place
   - **J.** in a bakery.
   - **K.** in a small town.
   - **L.** in the king's court.
   - **M.** in the town hall.

3. What lesson did the two bakers learn?
   - **A.** Baking bread is fun.
   - **B.** Working together brings success.
   - **C.** Keeping food on your shelves is important.
   - **D.** The king is always right.

4. The word "honor" means
   - **J.** king.
   - **K.** mayor.
   - **L.** recognition.
   - **M.** tradition.

Multiplication Practice

Complete the multiplication problems. The first one is done for you as an example.

Completa los problemas de multiplicación. El primer ya ha sido resuelto para usar como ejemplo.

```
              3
             12
1.     453           2.      94        3.      34        4.      24
     x  73               x  63             x  47             x  36
     1,359
  + 31,710
    33,069
```

```
5.      49           6.      73        7.      58        8.      27
     x  94               x  37             x  85             x  72
```

```
9.      19          10.      28       11.      37       12.      46
     x  85               x  76             x  18             x  89
```

```
13.     77          14.      76       15.      75       16.      74
     x  98               x  54             x  43             x  32
```

17. 63 x 57 = _____   **18.**   84 x 76 = _____

Getting to the Root of It

Sometimes a word has letters added to the beginning or end of it that change the meaning of the word. The main word is called the **root word**, and the added letters are **prefixes** and **suffixes**. For example, in the word *soundless* the root word is *sound*, and in the word *unusual* the root word is *usual*. Notice how the meanings of these two words change with the added letters.

*A veces las palabras tienen letras al comienzo o al final que cambian el significado de esa misma palabra. A la palabra principal se le llama **raíz**, y las letras añadidas son **prefijos** y **sufijos**. Por ejemplo, en la palabra "soundless" la palabra raíz es "sound" y en la palabra "unusual" la palabra raíz es "usual". Nota cómo cambia el significado con las letras añadidas.*

Read the words below. Write the root words in the spaces provided.

Lee las siguientes palabras. Escribe las palabras raíz en los espacios provistos.

1. irresponsible _____

2. misunderstand _____

3. meaningful _____

4. worthless _____

5. immaterial _____

6. disengage _____

7. unaware _____

8. prearrange _____

9. semicircle _____

10. biweekly _____

11. mountainous _____

12. unicycle _____

13. triangle _____

14. nonsense _____

15. admiralty _____

Plot, Setting, Characters

Read the story in the box below and answer the questions.

Lee el siguiente fragmento y luego responde las preguntas.

Chase is his baseball team's best pitcher. He can throw the ball really fast. However, Chase is the worst hitter. Everyone hits better than he does. Mike is the team's best hitter. Today, Chase's team needs just one run to win the game. It's Mike's turn to bat. Everyone thinks he will get a home run and win the game. Mike walks up to home plate and does a practice swing. He is sure he can hit the ball out of the park to win. A pitch is thrown, and Mike swings and misses. "Strike one!" the umpire calls. A second pitch is thrown, and Mike misses. No one can believe it when Mike swings at the last pitch and misses. Mike strikes out! Chase groans. He is next at bat. It is up to him. If he doesn't get a hit, the game will be over, and his team will lose. Chase drags his bat as he slowly walks to home plate. He doesn't even swing at the first pitch. He swings at the second pitch and misses. Chase looks at his teammates. He hates to disappoint them. He will try his best to hit the ball and get to first base. Then maybe the next batter can get a hit. The pitch is thrown. Chase swings and hears a crack. He begins to run to first base as he watches the ball. It flies over the fence. Chase can't believe it. He hit a home run. The crowd cheers, and his team waits for him at home plate. He is the hero of today's game.

Fluency Goal: Read 120 words in one minute. The highlighted word is the 120th word in the passage. See pages 12 and 13 for information on fluency.

Meta para la fluidez: Leer 120 palabras en un minuto. La palabra destacada es la palabra número 120 en la historia. Ver las páginas 12 y 13 para más información sobre la fluidez de la lectura.

1. Where and when does the story take place?
   A. backyard today
   B. ballpark on Saturday
   C. backyard on Saturday
   D. ballpark today

2. Who is the main character?
   A. the umpire
   B. Mike
   C. Chase
   D. the team

3. Who does everyone think will win the game for the team?
   A. the umpire
   B. Mike
   C. Chase
   D. Anthony

4. How many runs does the team need to win the game?
   A. one
   B. two
   C. three
   D. four

Perimeter Practice

- To compute the perimeter of a rectangle, add two adjoining sides and multiply the sum by 2.
- Perimeter = (length + width) x 2
- $P = (l + w)$ x 2

- Para encontrar el perímetro de un rectángulo, suma lo largo con lo ancho y multiplícalo por 2.
- Perímetro = (largo + ancho) x 2
- $P = (l + a)$ x 2

6 cm

2 cm

$P = (2 + 6)$ x 2
$P = 16$ cm

Compute the perimeter of each rectangle.

Calcula el perímetro de cada rectángulo.

1.　　　5 cm

4 cm

$P =$ _____

4.　　　9 in.

5 in.

$P =$ _____

7.　　　7 cm

4 cm

$P =$ _____

2.　　　8 cm

3 cm

$P =$ _____

5.　　　12 mm

9 mm

$P =$ _____

8.　　　13 cm

6 cm

$P =$ _____

3.　　　4 in.

3 in.

$P =$ _____

6.　　　18 mm

10 mm

$P =$ _____

9.　　　8 in.

6 in.

$P =$ _____

Possessives

Possessive nouns show who or what owns something. Singular possessive nouns are made by adding an apostrophe and then an s (the dog's bone). Plural possessive nouns are formed by adding an apostrophe after the s (the dogs' bones). However, when a plural noun does not end with an s, an apostrophe and then an s are added.

*Los **sustantivos posesivos** muestran quién o qué posee algo. Los sustantivos posesivos singulares se forman al añadir un apóstrofo y después una s (the dog's bone). Los sustantivos posesivos plurales se forman al añadir un apóstrofo después de la s (the dogs' bones). Cuando un sustantivo plural no termina en s, un apóstrofo y después una s son añadidos.*

Rewrite the underlined nouns in the sentences to make them possessive. (Possessive nouns function in sentences as adjectives. They describe other nouns.)

Vuelve a escribir los sustantivos subrayados en las oraciones para que sean posesivos. (Los sustantivos posesivos funcionan en las oraciones como adjetivos. Describen a otros sustantivos.)

1. The <u>doll</u> dress tore on the carriage. _____

2. <u>Lena</u> ball went over the fence. _____

3. Those <u>girls</u> jumping rope was tangled. _____

4. The <u>turtle</u> shell is like a home. _____

5. <u>Kate</u> mother brought her skates to the party. _____

6. The lost <u>child</u> father was relieved to find him. _____

7. The <u>boys</u> kites flew away. _____

8. The <u>penguin</u> baby cuddled against its mother. _____

9. The <u>blouse</u> button came loose. _____

10. The <u>pan</u> handle was very hot. _____

11. That <u>man</u> car is parked in the wrong place! _____

12. <u>Jen</u> homework is late. _____

13. The <u>lions</u> cage is near the tigers. _____

14. My <u>toys</u> cupboard needs to be cleaned. _____

15. The <u>play</u> cast was ready for opening night. _____

How Do You Make a Hot Dog Stand?

The answer to this riddle is written in a special code at the bottom of this page. Each pair of numbers stands for a point on the graph. Write the letter shown at the point near the intersection of each pair of numbers. Read numbers across and then up. The letters will spell out the answer to the riddle.

La respuesta a esta adivinanza está escrita en un código especial al final de la página. Cada par de números representa un punto de la gráfica. Escribe la letra que aparece en el punto cerca de la intersección de cada par de números. Lee los números de un lado a otro y luego hacia arriba. Las letras formarán la respuesta al acertijo.

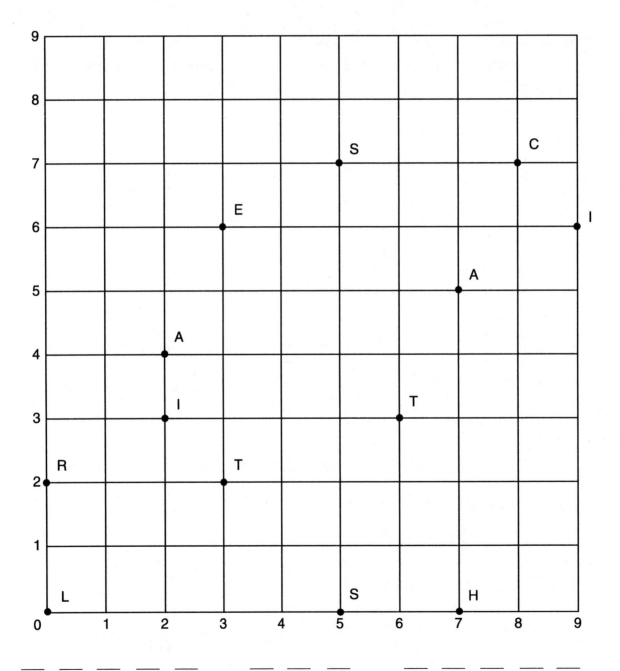

___ ___ ___ ___ ___   ___ ___ ___   ___ ___ ___ ___ ___
(5,7) (6,3) (3,6) (7,5) (0,0)   (2,3) (3,2) (5,0)   (8,7) (7,0) (2,4) (9,6) (0,2)

More Thesaurus Practice

Here is an entry from a thesaurus. Use it to answer the questions.

Aquí está una entrada de un tesauro. Úsala para contestar las preguntas.

---

bar: *n.* 1. strip, stake, stick, pole, rail, lever, rod, shaft, slab

2. tavern, saloon, counter, canteen, restaurant, snack bar, pub

bar: v. 1. barricade, dam, fence, wall, erect a barrier, shut or lock out, plug, seal, outlaw

2. ban, forbid, deny, refuse, reject

Ant. allow, admit, welcome

3. shut, lock, seal

---

1. You can infer from this thesaurus entry that a bar
    A. is a crooked piece of metal
    B. is an open door
    C. lets things happen
    D. can be a place to get something to eat or drink

Read this sentence.
Lee esta oración.

The workmen used a <u>bar</u> to strengthen the concrete.

---

2. Which *synonym* could be used to replace the word <u>bar</u> in the sentence?
    A. rod
    B. canteen
    C. outlaw
    D. refuse

Read this sentence.
Lee esta oración.

We <u>bar</u> people with backpacks from our store.

---

3. Which *antonym* could be used to replace the word <u>bar</u> in the sentence?
    A. welcome
    B. forbid
    C. reject
    D. shut out

It's All Relative

In the following sentences, circle the letters that need to be changed to capitals and write the capital letters above each one. If there is a capitalized word that should not be capitalized, draw a line through the appropriate letter.

En las siguientes oraciones, encierra en un círculo las letras que deben escribirse con mayúscula y escríbelas arriba de cada una. Si hay una mayúscula que debería ser minúscula, traza una línea a través de la letra correcta.

1. Uncle Jorge sat on the front Porch.

2. I said, "mom, what I really want to do is stay home!"

3. My mom and my dad won't be home until 7 P.M.

4. His grandma made a quilt for his birthday.

5. My Cousin and my Grandma will be coming with my mom.

6. Our Grandparents have a surprise for Aunt Aimee.

7. I wrote "Dear grandma," at the top of my stationery.

8. I wish my aunt lived closer to us; she looks just like mom.

9. Then dad stopped and looked behind him.

10. I like to go to grandmother Norton's house in the summer.

11. My favorite Cousin is Jimmy because he makes me laugh.

12. At the wedding we saw aunt Marsha and cousin Brad.

13. My Mom and Dad are taking me to dinner after the awards assembly.

14. At the reunion I saw Aunt Edith and uncle Jacques, and Cousins Kathy, Meredith, Hector, and Samantha.

15. For my birthday I'm inviting cousin Sarah, Cousin Leigh, aunt Susie, and my uncle, whose name is Mike.

Number Sequences

Determine the missing numbers in each sequence below.

Determina los números que faltan en cada una de las siguientes secuencias.

1. (2, 4, 6, 8, 10, 12, _____, _____, _____, _____, _____)

2. (1, 3, 5, 7, 9, 11, _____, _____, _____, _____, _____)

3. (1, 4, 7, 10, 13, _____, _____, _____, _____, _____)

4. (0, 3, 6, 9, 12, _____, _____, _____, _____, _____)

5. (0, 5, 10, 15, 20, 25, _____, _____, _____, _____, _____)

6. (7, 14, 21, 28, _____, _____, _____, _____, _____)

7. (22, 20, 18, 16, _____, _____, _____, _____, _____)

8. (97, 90, 83, 76, 69, 62, _____, _____, _____, _____, _____)

9. (100, 90, 80, _____, 60, _____, _____, _____, _____)

10. (27, 37, 47, _____, 67, _____, _____, _____, _____, _____)

11. (11, 22, 33, _____, 55, _____, _____, _____, _____, _____)

12. (2, 4, 8, 16, _____, _____, _____, _____, _____)

13. (3, 6, 12, _____, 48, _____, _____, _____, _____)

14. (25, 50, 75, 100, _____, _____, _____, _____, _____)

Challenge Project for Week 4

Make a family chart on a large piece of butcher paper. Put your name and a picture of yourself (a photograph or a self-drawn portrait) in the proper position. If you have brothers and/or sisters, add their names (and pictures if you wish). Add names below yours. Make as many lines as you need to represent your grandparents, aunts, uncles, and cousins. Be sure the lines appear in logical positions. A sample diagram appears below.

Haz una tabla familiar en una hoja grande de papel. Escribe tu nombre y haz un dibujo de ti miso (una fotografía o un dibujo de ti mismo) en la posición apropiada. Si tienes hermanos y hermanas, añade sus nombres (y fotos si lo deseas). Agrega nombres bajo el tuyo. Haz tantas líneas como ocupes para representar a tus abuelos, tías, tíos, y primos. Asegúrate que las líneas estén en posiciones lógicas. Hay un diagrama como ejemplo enseguida.

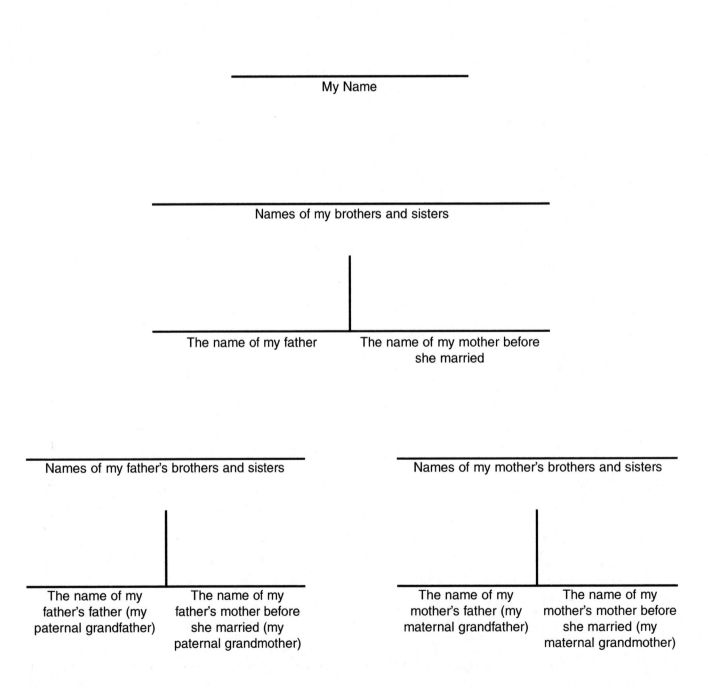

My Name

Names of my brothers and sisters

The name of my father   The name of my mother before she married

Names of my father's brothers and sisters   Names of my mother's brothers and sisters

The name of my father's father (my paternal grandfather)   The name of my father's mother before she married (my paternal grandmother)   The name of my mother's father (my maternal grandfather)   The name of my mother's mother before she married (my maternal grandmother)

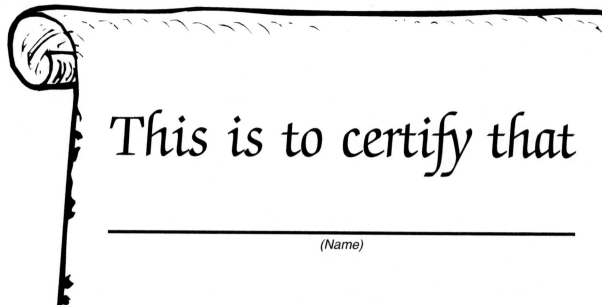

This is to certify that

_____
(Name)

finished all the activity sheets for week 4.

Congratulations!

_____
(Date)

Favorite Teams

Five boys root for five different baseball teams. Read the clues to determine which team each likes best. Mark the correct boxes with an **X**.

*Cinco niños alientan a cinco equipos de béisbol distintos. Lee las pistas para determinar qué equipo le gusta más a cada uno. Marca los cuadros correctos con una **X**.*

1. Will's bedroom is filled with posters and products from the A's.

2. Andrew's father is a big Cardinals fan, but Andrew is not.

3. Chad and Ryan like the Dodgers, the Reds, or the A's.

4. No boy's favorite team begins with the same letter as his name.

	Cardinals	Dodgers	A's	Reds	White Sox
Chad					
Danny					
Andrew					
Ryan					
Will					

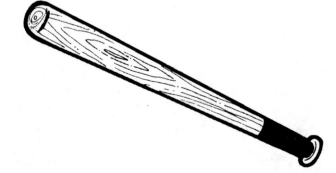

Keeping Questions in Mind

Read the passages, then answer the questions.

Después de leer el fragmento, completa las siguientes preguntas.

Passage 1

The Constitutional Convention was a meeting held in Philadelphia, Pennsylvania. It began in May of 1787 and lasted nearly four months. Each state—except for Rhode Island—sent a representative. Sometimes these men agreed and other times they disagreed. They argued and made changes. Step by step they wrote the United States Constitution. Today it is the supreme law of our land. It created the type of government we have and listed our basic rights.

Clerks used ink and feather quill pens to write the four pages of the Constitution. Then 39 men signed their names to it. This meant that they agreed with what it said. Some people believe that it is the most important document ever written. No wonder it took so long to write!

Find the answers in the passage.

Encuentra las respuestas en el texto.

Who or What?: _____ representatives from each state except Rhode Island _____

Did What?:_____

When?: _____

Where?:_____

Why?: _____

How?: _____

Passage 2

The Transcontinental Railroad allowed people to travel by train across the entire width of the U.S.A. Building it had taken years of work. Most of it had to be done by hand. The work was hard and often dangerous. Many men lost their lives blasting tunnels through mountains. Still, lots of men signed up to build the railroad.

Railroad crews started at each of America's coasts. One crew started laying tracks at the East Coast. They headed west as fast as they could. The other crew began laying tracks at the West Coast. They headed east as fast as they could. The crews met each other when the rails joined in Utah on May 10, 1869. A big celebration marked the railroad's completion.

Find the answers in the passage.

Encuentra las respuestas en el texto.

Who or What?: _____

Did What?:_____

When?: _____

Where?:_____

Why?: _____

How?: _____

What Does It Mean?

Many words have more than one meaning. When reading, you can use context clues to determine the meaning of a word in a sentence. Read the sentences below and then write the letter of the definition that shows how the underlined word is used in each sentence.

Muchas palabras tienen más de un significado. Cuando leas, puedes usar las pistas del contexto para determinar el significado de una palabra en una oración. Lee las siguientes oraciones y después escribe la letra de la definición que muestra cómo se usa la palabra subrayada en cada oración.

_____ 1. Tell me your <u>address</u> so I can find where you live.

    a. speak or write to

    b. manner of speech

    c. place where a person lives

_____ 2. Why do you <u>refuse</u> to come to the fair?

    a. decline to accept

    b. garbage

    c. decline to do

_____ 3. Lost in the <u>desert</u> for hours, the people were hot, hungry, and thirsty.

    a. dry, sandy wasteland

    b. abandon

    c. something deserved

_____ 4. The children at <u>play</u> were running and laughing with joy.

    a. put in motion

    b. taking part in a game or recreation

    c. a dramatic work

_____ 5. Are there any cookies <u>left</u> for me?

    a. the westward direction when one is facing north

    b. remaining

    c. departed

Reading a Recipe

Read the recipe in the box below and answer the questions.

Lee el fragmento y luego responde a las preguntas a continuación.

Apricot Banana Shake

Food You Will Need:
- 1 cup orange juice, chilled
- 1/2 cup milk
- 1/4 teaspoon vanilla
- 1 16-ounce can pitted apricot halves, chilled
- 1 banana
- ground nutmeg

Equipment You Will Need:
- measuring cups
- can opener
- blender
- drinking glasses

Directions:

1. Measure the orange juice, milk, and vanilla into the blender. Add the apricots and their juice. Peel the banana. Break the banana into four pieces; add to the blender container.

2. With help from an adult, put the lid on the blender and blend the mixture until it is smooth. Pour the mixture into the glasses; sprinkle the top with a little nutmeg.

Serve cold and enjoy. Makes 4 servings.

To make your table look special, add a vase of flowers and tie pretty bows around some colorful paper napkins. Use rusts, greens, and browns in the fall. A winter table looks nice with reds and greens and pine cones with ivy or greens from trees. Soft colors and small bunny decorations work well in the spring. Try any flower and color together during the summer. Red, white, and blue ideas make a perfect table for the 4th of July.

---

1. To make sure you know how to make the shake,

  A. read a story about a summer party.

  B. read the entire recipe before making the shake.

  C. read a story about the inventor of apricot banana shakes.

  D. read an article about the 4th of July.

2. When should you add the apricots?

  J. after you peel the banana and break it into four pieces

  K. after you pour the mixture into the glasses

  L. after you set the table with a vase of flowers

  M. after you measure the orange juice, milk, and vanilla into the blender

3. How much milk do you need?

  A. 1/4 teaspoon   **B.** 1/2 cup

  C. 1 cup   **D.** 16 ounces

4. The recipe could also be called

  J. "How to Make Your Table Look Special."

  K. "How to Use a Blender."

  L. "A Tasty Treat for All Seasons."

  M. "How to Throw a Summer Party."

5. To make an apricot banana shake, you do not need a

  A. blender.   **B.** can opener.

  C. pumpkin.   **D.** banana.

6. The last paragraph was written mainly

  J. to show that the 4th of July is the best time to have a party.

  K. to show that apricot banana shakes should only be served on a table.

  L. to give ideas about how to decorate for the holidays.

  M. to show how to tie bows around paper napkins.

Division with Remainders

Complete the division problems. The first two are is done for you as examples.

Completa los problemas de división. Los primeros problemas ya han sido resueltos para usar como ejemplos.

```
        103  R3            77  R1
1.  4 )415          2.  3 )232          3.  5 )269          4.  3 )319
      - 4                 - 21
       15                  22
      - 12                - 21
        3                   1
```

5. 6)917   6. 9)263   7. 8)109   8. 2)327

9. 7)709   10. 4)419   11. 6)806   12. 4)818

13. 4)915   14. 4)729   15. 3)929   16. 5)951

Get Rid of the Extra Details

Read the paragraph below. It has too many details to be a summary. You must decide which words or phrases are not important enough to be in a short summary. Cross out the words or phrases that are not important details. To create a summarizing paragraph, copy the sentences and words you did not cross out.

Lee el párrafo siguiente. Tiene demasiados detalles para ser un resumen. Debes decidir qué palabras o frases no son suficientemente importantes para estar en un resumen corto. Tacha las palabras y frases que no son detalles importantes. Para crear un párrafo resumido, copia las oraciones y palabras que no tachaste.

Every animal has babies. Sometimes the mother takes care of the baby until it can take care of itself. Baby animals are cute. Sometimes the whole group of animals care for the babies. Baby bears are called cubs. The cubs like to eat honey. Baby animals must eat. Mothers and fathers protect their babies. Some baby animals, like kangaroos, live in pouches. Other baby animals travel on their mothers' backs. Possums and monkeys carry babies on their backs. Baby animals are fun to watch.

Summary

_____

_____

_____

_____

_____

_____

_____

Dreams

Describe a dream that you once had and draw a picture to go with it. Be sure to write complete sentences with subjects and predicates.

Describe un sueño que hayas tenido alguna vez y haz un dibujo que valla con él. Asegúrate de escribir oraciones completas son sujetos y predicados.

Which Is It?

Read the number sentences. Add the correct math sign to each problem.

Lee las oraciones numéricas. Agrega el signo matemático correcto para cada problema.

+ add	− subtract	× multiply	÷ divide

1. 5 _____ 7 = 12

2. 24 _____ 4 = 6

3. 9 _____ 3 = 12

4. 18 _____ 6 = 12

5. 4 _____ 9 = 13

6. 4 _____ 9 = 36

7. 10 _____ 8 = 80

8. 15 _____ 5 = 3

9. 11 _____ 4 = 7

10. 8 _____ 16 = 24

11. 2 _____ 8 = 16

12. 3 _____ 2 = 5

13. 22 _____ 6 = 16

14. 9 _____ 1 = 10

15. 3 _____ 3 = 9

16. 144 _____ 12 = 12

17. 21 _____ 3 = 7

18. 90 _____ 10 = 9

19. 12 _____ 11 = 132

20. 14 _____ 1 = 14

Movie Review

Using the lines below, write a review of your favorite movie or TV program. Remember to include details about the plot and descriptions of the characters. Give specific details to support your main idea.

En los siguientes renglones, escribe una reseña de tu película favorita. Recuerda incluir detalles sobre el argumento y descripciones de los personajes. Ofrece detalles específicos para respaldar tu idea principal.

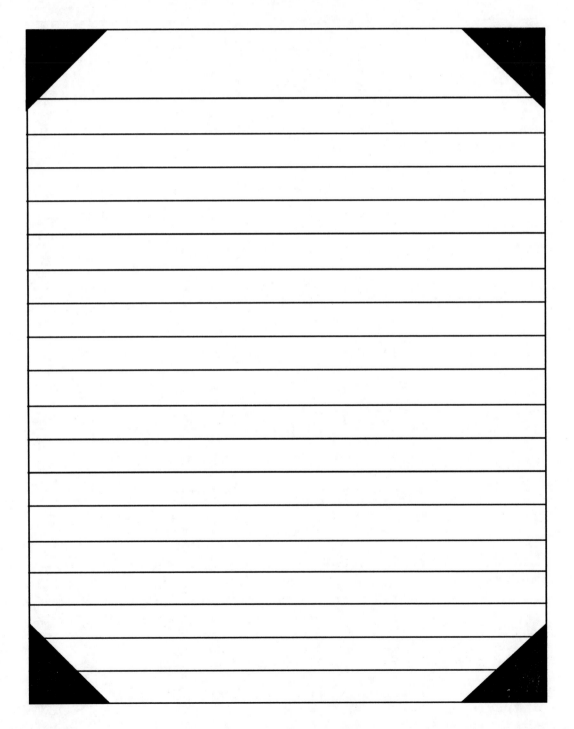

How Many Miles?

Use the map to answer the questions below.

Utiliza el mapa para contestar las preguntas siguientes.

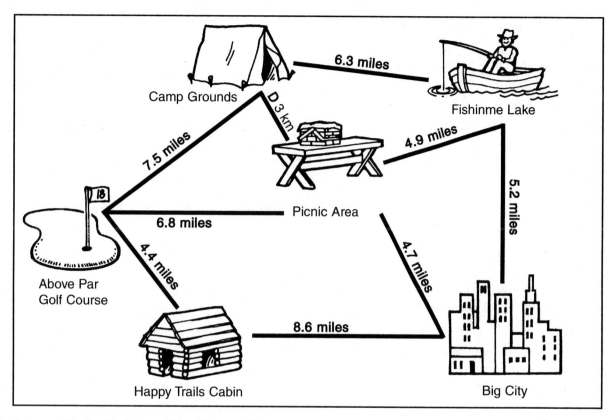

1. Happy Trails Cabin to Big City to Fishinme Lake   _____ mi.

2. Fishinme Lake to Picnic Area to Camp Grounds   _____ mi.

3. Above Par Golf Course to Camp Grounds to Big City   _____ mi.

List the different routes that could be taken to go from Above Par Golf Course to Fishinme Lake.

4. _____ = _____ mi.

5. _____ = _____ mi.

6. _____ = _____ mi.

7. _____ = _____ mi.

8. Which route is the longest? _____

9. Which route is the shortest? _____

10. Are there any routes that are about the same in distance? _____

Challenge Project for Week 5
Perimeter versus Area

Read the directions and help your child complete this project.

Lea las direcciones y ayude a su hijo a completar este proyecto.

Materials Needed:
- string or yarn (cuerda o hilo)
- graph paper from page 93 (papel gráfico de la página 93)
- piece of heavy cardboard larger than graph paper (pedazo de cartulina gruesa más grande que el papel gráfico)
- pins (optional) (alfileres – opcional)

1. Cut a piece of string or yarn 16 inches long. Put the ends together with tape without overlapping the ends of the string.

   Corta una pedazo de cuerda o hilo de 16 pulgadas de largo. Junta las puntas con un pedazo de cinta sin encimar las puntas de la cuerda.

2. Lay a piece of graph paper with 1-inch (2.5 cm) squares (page 93) on top of a piece of heavy cardboard.

   Coloca un pedazo de papel gráfico (pagina 93) de cuadros de una pulgada (2.5 cm) encima de un pedazo grueso de cartulina.

3. Lay the piece of string on the graph paper so that it forms a square with 4-inch (10.2 cm) sides. Use pins to hold the corners, if needed.

   Coloca el pedazo de hilo sobre el papel gráfico de manera que forme un cuadrado con lados de 4 pulgadas (10.2 cm). Usa los alfileres para asegurar las esquinas si necesitas.

4. You already know the perimeter of the square because you cut the string to be 16 inches long. (Count the squares inside the string on the graph paper and write the number.) That is the area of the square.

   Ya sabes el perímetro del cuadrado porque cortaste el hilo de 16 pulgadas de largo. (Cuenta los cuadros dentro del hilo en el papel gráfico y apunta el número.) Esta es el área del cuadrado.

5. Now, lay the string so it forms a rectangle 7 inches long and 1 inch wide. Use pins to hold the corners and draw around the rectangle you just made.

   Ahora, coloca el hilo para que forme un rectángulo de 7 pulgadas de largo y 1 pulgada de ancho. Usa alfileres para asegurar las esquinas y traza el rectángulo que acabas de formar.

6. You already know the perimeter of the rectangle because you are still using the string that you cut to be 16 inches long. What is the area of this rectangle? (Count the squares inside the string on the graph paper and write the number.)

   Ya sabes el perímetro del rectángulo porque estas usando el hilo de 16 pulgadas de largo. ¿Cuál es el área de este rectángulo? (Cuenta los cuadros dentro del hilo en el papel gráfico y apunta el número.)

7. Do this whole experiment over again, making a rectangle that is 6 inches long and 2 inches wide. What is the area?

   Haz el experimento otra vez, haciendo un rectángulo que sea 6 pulgadas de largo y 2 pulgadas de ancho. ¿Cuál es el área?

8. Try the experiment with strings of different lengths.

   Trata de hacer el experimento con hilos de diferentes tamaños.

9. Think about the results you found. What conclusions can you draw about perimeter and area?

   Piensa en los resultados que obtuviste. ¿Qué conclusiones puedes obtener sobre el perímetro y el área?

Certificate of Achievement

This is to certify that

_____
(Name)

worked hard to finish all the activity sheets for week 5.
This effort is to be commended.

_____
(Date)

Terrific!

Marta and Janis

Read the story. Then use the lines under the story to write how the two friends are the same and how they are different from each other.

Lee la historia. Después usa los renglones debajo de ella para escribir en qué se parecen las dos amigas y en qué se diferencian.

Marta and Janis are both eight years old. They have been best friends for two years, even though Marta does not speak much English. Marta is from Mexico. She speaks Spanish very well, a language that Janis does not understand. Marta is teaching Janis to speak Spanish, and Janis is helping Marta to speak better English.

Every afternoon, the girls do their homework together. They munch on their favorite snack, popcorn. Sometimes Janis has to bring her little brother along. He colors in his coloring book while the girls study. Marta loves little Pete, and she wishes she had a baby brother or sister.

After they finish their homework, Marta and Janis go to the city park. Marta takes her skates. She is a wonderful skater. Janis brings her scooter. She loves to ride. When Pete comes along, all the children swing and slide. They all enjoy that! It is good to have a best friend!

Fluency Goal: Read 120 words in one minute. The highlighted word is the 120th word in the passage. See pages 12 and 13 for information on fluency.

Meta para la fluidez: *Leer 120 palabras en un minuto. La palabra destacada es la palabra número 120 en la historia. Ver las páginas 12 y 13 para más información sobre la fluidez de la lectura.*

1. How are Marta and Janis alike?

_____

_____

_____

_____

_____

2. How are Marta and Janis different?

_____

_____

_____

_____

_____

Working with Fractions

Adding and subtracting fractions is easy when the denominators (bottom numbers) are the same. Simply add or subtract the numerators (top numbers).

Sumar y restar fracciones es fácil cuando los denominadores (los números abajo) son iguales. Simplemente suma o resta los numeradores (los números arriba).

Examples: $\dfrac{1}{4} + \dfrac{2}{4} = \dfrac{3}{4}$ $\dfrac{5}{7} - \dfrac{1}{7} = \dfrac{4}{7}$

Add or subtract the fractions below.

Suma o resta las fracciones siguientes.

1. $\dfrac{3}{4} - \dfrac{2}{4} =$ _____

2. $\dfrac{2}{5} + \dfrac{1}{5} =$ _____

3. $\dfrac{3}{6} + \dfrac{2}{6} =$ _____

4. $\dfrac{2}{9} + \dfrac{6}{9} =$ _____

5. $\dfrac{5}{7} - \dfrac{3}{7} =$ _____

6. $\dfrac{8}{9} - \dfrac{4}{9} =$ _____

7. $\dfrac{2}{4} + \dfrac{1}{4} =$ _____

8. $\dfrac{2}{9} + \dfrac{3}{9} =$ _____

9. $\dfrac{2}{3} - \dfrac{1}{3} =$ _____

10. $\dfrac{5}{8} - \dfrac{1}{8} =$ _____

11. $\dfrac{3}{9} - \dfrac{1}{9} =$ _____

12. $\dfrac{4}{8} - \dfrac{2}{8} =$ _____

13. $\dfrac{1}{6} + \dfrac{4}{6} =$ _____

14. $\dfrac{1}{7} + \dfrac{3}{7} =$ _____

15. $\dfrac{5}{9} + \dfrac{2}{9} =$ _____

Read and solve each word problem.

Lee y resuelve cada problema escrito.

16. The recipe calls for $\dfrac{1}{4}$ of a cup of brown sugar and $\dfrac{1}{4}$ of a cup of white sugar. How much sugar is needed in all?

_____ of a cup of sugar

17. In a glass, Dave mixed $\dfrac{1}{5}$ of a cup of chocolate milk with $\dfrac{2}{5}$ of a cup of white milk. How much liquid is in the glass?

_____ of a cup of liquid

18. Cher used $\dfrac{1}{3}$ of a cup of red jellybeans and $\dfrac{1}{3}$ of a cup of green jellybeans. How much did she use in all?

_____ of a cup in all

19. To make the dressing, pour $\dfrac{1}{5}$ of a cup of vinegar and $\dfrac{3}{5}$ of a cup of oil into a bowl. How much dressing is made?

_____ of a cup of dressing

I Will Convince You

A **persuasive paragraph** is what you write when you express an opinion and try to convince the reader that your opinion is correct. Think of how you try to persuade a parent to buy your favorite cereal or a new pair of shoes that you are convinced you must have. You may be convinced, but you will need to work hard to persuade others. To persuade, you will need lots of *examples, details*, and *evidence to prove your point*.

Un párrafo persuasivo es lo que escribes cuando expresas una opinión y tratas de convencer al lector que tu opinión es correcta. Piensa en cómo tratas de persuadir a uno de tus padres para que te compren tu cereal favorito o un par de zapatos nuevos de los que estás convencido que tienes que obtener. Quizás tú estés convencido, pero necesitaras trabajar duro para persuadir a otros. Para persuadir, necesitas muchos ejemplos, detalles y evidencia para demostrar tu punto.

Here is an example of a persuasive paragraph.   **Aquí hay un ejemplo de un párrafo persuasivo.**

> Everybody needs to have a pet. Have you ever noticed that people who do not have pets are grouchier than those who do? If they were greeted whenever they came home by a furry creature thrilled to see them, they would be a lot less grouchy. A pet is affectionate and a good companion. Pets like to snuggle and be with people. Also, pets are always positive. If you give them a special treat, they act as if you've given them the world's largest diamond or the fastest car. They shudder with joy, leap, and prance. If you've had a hard day, they still greet you with enthusiasm. They don't care what you do. You can be a complete failure, and they still treat you as if you are a king or queen. Pets love you unconditionally. If you forget to feed them, they forgive you the moment you remember. Pets are also good safety devices. They can scare away strangers. They can warn you if there is a fire or something wrong inside or outside the house. All they ask in return is a bag of food, some water, and some TLC (tender, loving care). If everybody had a pet, everybody would go around smiling.

Fluency Goal: Read 120 words in one minute. The highlighted word is the 120th word in the passage. See pages 12 and 13 for information on fluency.

Meta para la fluidez: Leer 120 palabras en un minuto. La palabra destacada es la palabra número 120 en la historia. Ver las páginas 12 y 13 para más información sobre la fluidez de la lectura.

Choose a topic below or create your own topic and, on a separate piece of paper, write a persuasive paragraph. Remember to be as convincing as you can.

Elige uno de los siguientes temas o crea tu propio tema y, en una hoja aparte, escribe un párrafo persuasivo. Trata de ser lo más convincente que puedas.

- ❏ Pets are a waste of time and money.
- ❏ We should continue to explore space.
- ❏ Space exploration is not a good use of our money.
- ❏ Libraries are invaluable.
- ❏ Bookstores are better than libraries.
- ❏ People should always have dessert.
- ❏ Desserts should be banned.
- ❏ Everybody should play a sport.

- ❏ Sports are overrated.
- ❏ Jewelry is fun.
- ❏ Jewelry is expensive.
- ❏ Students should wear uniforms to school.
- ❏ Students should be allowed to dress the way they want.
- ❏ We should have more zoos.
- ❏ We should do away with zoos.

Evaluating Bias

Facts tell only what can be proven. Biased statements tell a person's **opinion**. Write **F** for fact or **O** for opinion on the line before each statement.

*Los **hechos** dicen sólo lo que puede ser comprobado. Las declaraciones prejudiciales dicen **opiniones** personales. Escribe **F** para hecho o **O** para opinión en la linea antes de cada oración.*

_____ 1. Lions roar loudly.

_____ 2. Pigs are the laziest of all animals.

_____ 3. Horses must be brushed often to keep them clean.

_____ 4. Dogs are better pets than cats.

_____ 5. The Riverside Zoo was built three years ago.

_____ 6. More than 400 animals live in the Riverside Zoo.

_____ 7. The Riverside Zoo is the best zoo in the world.

_____ 8. The emperor penguin is the most interesting animal to watch.

_____ 9. Snakes should not be allowed at the zoo because they frighten visitors.

_____10. Polar bears are large, white animals.

Problem Solving

Solve the problems. You will need to estimate some answers.

Resuelve los problemas. Vas a necesitar estimar algunas de las repuestas.

Example
Jocelyn ran in 3 cross-country events. She received **321**, **489**, and **273 points. About how many** points **all together** did Jocelyn earn?

A 900
B 1,000
C 1,100
D 1,200

1.

The same number of cats were curled up on each of **5 chairs**. A total of **45 cats** were curled up on these chairs. **How many** cats were **on each chair?**

A 7
B 9
C 40
D 50

---

2. John's fishing boat caught **2,735 pounds** of fish. They **put** them **into boxes of 92 pounds each. About how many boxes** did they **need?**

J 3   M 3000
K 30   O 90
L 300

---

3. Shari wondered about how much her cat weighed. **Which** is **most likely** his **weight?**

A 12 tons
B 12 ounces
C 12 pounds
D 12 quarts

---

4. Choose the answer that is **not** a **prime number**.

23   17   16   5
J   K   L   M

---

5. Ann played Math Martians on her computer. She **scored 832** in the first game, **505** in the second, and **397** in her last game. **About how many** points **all together** did she earn?

A 1,900
B 1,800
C 1,700
D 1,600

Identifying and Using Pronouns

Pronouns are words that are used in place of nouns. Like nouns, personal pronouns are used as both subjects and objects in sentences.

Los pronombres son palabras usadas para reemplazar los susantivos. Como los sustantivos, los pronombres personales son usados como ambos sujetos y objectos en las oraciones.

Rewrite the sentences below using personal pronouns (I, you, he, she, it, we, they, me, him, her, us, them) to replace the nouns in bold print.

Vuelve a escribir estas oraciones usando pronombres personales (I, you, he, she, it, we, they, me, him, her, us, them) para sustituir los sustantivos en negritas.

1. **Luke** played baseball. _____

2. Mom read **the new bestseller**. _____

3. **Lucille** swam across the pool. _____

4. **The girls** walked to Mary's house. _____

5. **Lucille and Luke** climbed trees. _____

6. The team gave **Lucille** a trophy. _____

7. Rosa saw **the dog** run away. _____

8. **My dad** put gas in the car. _____

9. Ricardo saw **the strange man**. _____

10. Where is **the key**? _____

11. **The key** is here! _____

12. Where should I put **the presents**? _____

13. **Rosa** put the presents away. _____

14. Ricardo, give this to **Rosa**. _____

15. **Lucille** is coming to my house. _____

16. I gave **Luke** the book to read. _____

17. **Rosa and I** are wearing dresses. _____

18. Are **Rosa and Luke** at home? _____

19. **The book** is on the table. _____

20. **Ricardo and his friends** arrived. _____

What a Success!

Imagine that one day you become very famous. Write a story about the success that brings you fame. Give your story a title. In the story, explain how and why you became famous. Also tell about what other important things you might do in the future.

Imagina que un día te haces famoso. Escribe una historia sobre el éxito que te llevo a la fama. Ponle un título a tu historia. En la historia, explica cómo y por qué te hiciste famoso. También cuenta sobre qué otras cosas importantes harás en el futuro.

_____

_____

_____

_____

_____

_____

_____

_____

_____

_____

_____

_____

_____

_____

_____

_____

_____

_____

_____

Opposites Attract

Antonyms are words that mean the opposite of each other. For example: *good* and *bad, quiet* and *noisy.*

Los antónimos son palabras que tienen significados opuestos. Por ejemplo: bueno y malo, callado y ruidoso.

Look at the words in column 1. Find the antonym for each word in column 2. Write the letter of the antonym in column 2 next to its match in column 1. The first one has been done for you.

Observa las palabras de la columna 1. Encuentra el antónimo de cada una en la columna 2. Escribe la letra del antónimo de la columna 2 junto a la palabra que le corresponde de la columna 1. El primero ya está hecho.

Column 1

___F___ 1. accept

_____ 2. bury

_____ 3. crooked

_____ 4. disgust

_____ 5. familiar

_____ 6. gloomy

_____ 7. hungry

_____ 8. locate

_____ 9. mysterious

_____ 10. nonsense

_____ 11. obey

_____ 12. pride

_____ 13. quit

_____ 14. responsible

_____ 15. slender

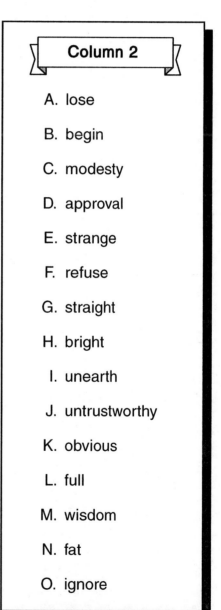

Column 2

A. lose

B. begin

C. modesty

D. approval

E. strange

F. refuse

G. straight

H. bright

I. unearth

J. untrustworthy

K. obvious

L. full

M. wisdom

N. fat

O. ignore

Choose three antonym pairs. On another piece of paper, write sentences that include both words.

Escoge tres pares de antónimos. En otra hoja de papel, escribe oraciones que incluyan ambas palabras.

Using Grids

A grid is an arrangement of blocks that are made by vertical and horizontal lines intersecting on a page. Numbers and letters are used on the grid to help you name the blocks. You can find something on a grid by putting a finger of your right hand on a number and a finger of your left hand on a letter. Then, slide your fingers together until they meet. When grid points are identified, the letter is written before the number.

Cuadrícula es el arreglo de bloques que son hechos por líneas horizontales y verticales que se juntan en una hoja. Números y letras pueden ser usados en una cuadrícula para ayudarte a nombrar los bloques. Puedes encontrar algo en una cuadrícula colocando un dedo de tu mano derecha sobre un número y un dedo de tu mano izquierda sobre una letra. Después desliza tus dedos hasta que se junten. Cuando puntos en una cuadrícula son identificados, la letra se escribe antes que el número.

Grid X

	1	2	3	4
A	white	yellow	orange	gold
B	pink	green	tan	red
C	blue	purple	brown	silver
D	black	ivory	gray	lavender

Grid Y

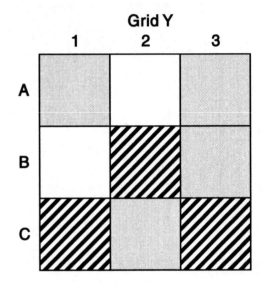

1. Use grid X to name each of the following colors:

   Usa la cuadrícula X para nombrar cada uno de los siguientes colores:

   A1 _____   D3 _____   B4 _____   D2 _____

   C4 _____   A2 _____   D1 _____   C2 _____

   B3 _____   A4 _____   C3 _____   B1 _____

   D4 _____   B2 _____   A3 _____   C1 _____

2. Use grid Y to answer these questions.

   Usa la cuadrícula Y para responder a estas preguntas.

   a. Which blocks are shaded?   _____

   b. Which blocks are striped?   _____

   c. Which blocks are unmarked?   _____

Comprehension Assessment

Read the passage below and circle the letters of the correct answers to the questions.

Lee el siguiente texto y luego encierra en un círculo las letras de las respuestas correctas a las preguntas.

The tribe had but one problem: a steady supply of fresh water. Everyone needed water for drinking, cooking, and cleaning. Yet the nearby stream to which the women carried their water jugs each day would sometimes abruptly stop flowing. There was neither rhyme nor reason to the dry spells. No one could predict them, for there was never any warning. Sometimes the problem lasted for days, other times for weeks. Whenever it happened, the women of the tribe had to spend most of their day walking to and from a distant pool. Nobody actually knew why this kept happening.

On the day our story begins, the women took their water jugs to fill them. When they reached the stream, however, they found it all but empty. Shallow depressions held small, muddy puddles of water, but even those would disappear under the sun's scorching rays. The women split into two groups. One group followed the stream to see if any water could be found further downstream. The other followed the stream to look for water upstream. But just as every time before, none could be found anywhere.

Fluency Goal: Read 120 words in one minute. The highlighted word is the 120th word in the passage. See pages 12 and 13 for information on fluency.

Meta para la fluidez: Leer 120 palabras en un minuto. La palabra destacada es la palabra número 120 en la historia. Ver las páginas 12 y 13 para más información sobre la fluidez de la lectura.

1. What is the main idea?
   a Sometimes the stream is dry, but nobody knows why.
   b A magic spell has been placed on the stream that the tribe relies upon for water.
   c The women of the tribe must carry water to the village.
   d The tribe can never get enough water from a nearby stream.

2. What is the topic sentence of the first paragraph?
   a Shallow depressions held small, muddy puddles of water, but even those would disappear under the sun's scorching rays.
   b On the day our story begins, the women took their water jugs to fill them.
   c There was neither rhyme nor reason to the dry spells.
   d The tribe had but one problem: a steady supply of fresh water.

3. What is the best title for this passage?
   a A Tribe with a Problem
   b The Mysterious Stream
   c The Thirsty Tribe
   d Muddy Water Misery

Challenge Project for Week 6

An idiom is a phrase that is a figure of speech. If idioms are taken literally they either do not make sense or are extremely silly. For example, you may have heard the idiom, "It's raining cats and dogs." This phrase does not mean that cats and dogs are really falling out of the sky. It means that it is raining very hard. It is important to learn about idioms because they are often used in speaking and in books to describe things or events.

Un refrán es una frase que asimila las cosas. Si los refranes son tomados literalmente no tienen sentido o son extremadamente chistosos. Por ejemplo, habrás escuchado el modismo que dice, "están lloviendo perros y gatos". Esta frase no significa que perros y gatos están realmente cayendo del cielo. Significa que está lloviendo muy fuerte. Es importante aprender sobre los refranes porque son usados a menudo cuando se habla y en libros para describir eventos.

Listed below are many common idioms. Choose three idioms and follow the directions below for each.

Enseguida hay una lista de muchos refranes comunes. Escoge tres refranes y sigue las direcciones siguientes para cada uno.

- She's a back seat driver.
- Break a leg!
- Don't count your chickens before they hatch.
- He got up on the wrong side of the bed.
- He's feeling under the weather.
- Hold your horses.
- Put on your thinking cap.
- Right from the horses mouth.
- She let the cat out of the bag.

- She's running around like a chicken with its head cut off.
- Take that to the bank.
- That was a piece of cake.
- That's for the birds.
- The apple doesn't fall far from the tree.
- The early bird catches the worm.
- You are what you eat.

1. Write the idiom across the top of a piece of white paper as the title.

   Escribe el refrán en el centro de la parte superior de una hoja en blanco como título.

2. Fold the piece of paper in half and then fold in half again, so that there are four sections. Number the sections from one to four.

   Dobla la pieza de papel por la mitad y después dóblala otra vez, para que haya cuatro secciones. Numera las secciones del uno al cuatro.

3. In the first section, draw a literal picture of the idiom. For example, if the phrase is It's raining cats and dogs, draw a picture of cats and dogs falling from the sky.

   En la primera sección, dibuja uno de los refranes literalmente. Por ejemplo, si la frase dice están lloviendo perros y gatos, puedes dibujar perros y gatos cayendo del cielo.

4. In the second section, write a short paragraph about why this phrase cannot be taken literally. For example, It is not really possible for cats or dogs to fall from the sky like rain.

   En la segunda sección, escribe un párrafo corto sobre por qué esta frase no se puede tomar literalmente. Por ejemplo, no es posible que perros y gatos caigan del cielo como la lluvia.

5. In the third section, draw a picture of what the phrase really means. For example, a picture of extremely heavy rain falling from the sky.

   En la tercera sección, dibuja lo que realmente significa la frase. Por ejemplo, una foto de lluvia que cae extremadamente fuerte del cielo.

6. In the fourth section, write a short paragraph about what the phrase really means. For example, The idiom means that it's raining really hard.

   En la cuarta sección, escribe un párrafo corto sobre lo que la frase realmente significa. Por ejemplo, El modismo significa que está lloviendo muy fuerte.

7. Try to use the idiom in conversation sometime in the next few days.

   Trata de usar el modismo durante tus conversaciones en los siguientes días.

Outstanding!
Terrific!
Super-Fantastic!

This certifies that

_____

(Full Name)

has completed all the activity pages for week 6.

Good luck in Fifth Grade!

Outstanding Work

_____

(Parent)

_____

(Date)

High Frequency Words

Here is a list of high frequency words that you should be familiar with. Whenever you are writing sentences or paragraphs, reference this list to be sure you are spelling these words correctly.

Aquí hay una lista de las palabras más usadas con las que tienes que familiarizarte. Cuando escribas oraciones o párrafos, usa esta lista para asegurarte de que estás escribiendo estas palabras correctamente.

about	fast	lay	reason	took
above	few	learn	receive	toward
across	find	left	right	try
after	finished	light	run	turn
again	first	like	said	two
almost	five	little	same	under
already	found	long	sat	upon
always	four	look	saw	use
another	from	love	say	very
answer	full	made	short	visit
any	gave	main	side	walk
around	get	make	since	want
away	give	many	sit	warm
bad	going	mean	sky	was
because	gone	meet	small	weather
been	good	mind	soon	well
before	got	month	start	went
began	great	more	still	were
believe	grow	most	stop	what
beside	had	much	take	when
best	happy	must	teacher	where
better	hard	near	tell	whether
black	has	need	ten	which
both	have	never	than	while
bring	held	new	that	white
call	help	next	the	whose
came	her	now	their	why
cause	here	old	them	will
close	high	once	then	wish
cold	him	only	there	without
could	his	open	these	won't
describe	hold	other	they	work
didn't	hot	our	think	would
does	I'm	over	third	wrote
done	into	paint	this	yet
don't	its	past	those	you
down	just	picked	three	your
draw	keep	play	through	
during	know	probably	today	
every	last	read	told	

One-Inch Graph Paper

Tear out this page and use it for the Challenge Activity on page 78.

Corta esta hoja y úsala para el proyecto de desafió de la pagina 78.

(This page is left blank so you can cut out the manipulative on the previous page.)

(Esta página está en blanco para permitirle cortar el manipulativo de la página anterior.)

Number Line (-100– 100)

Cut along the dashed lines. Tape the number line together, edge to edge, with no overlap.
Use it when adding or subtracting.

Corta las líneas marcadas. Pega la línea numérica de lado a lado sin encimarlas. Úsala cuando sumes o restes.

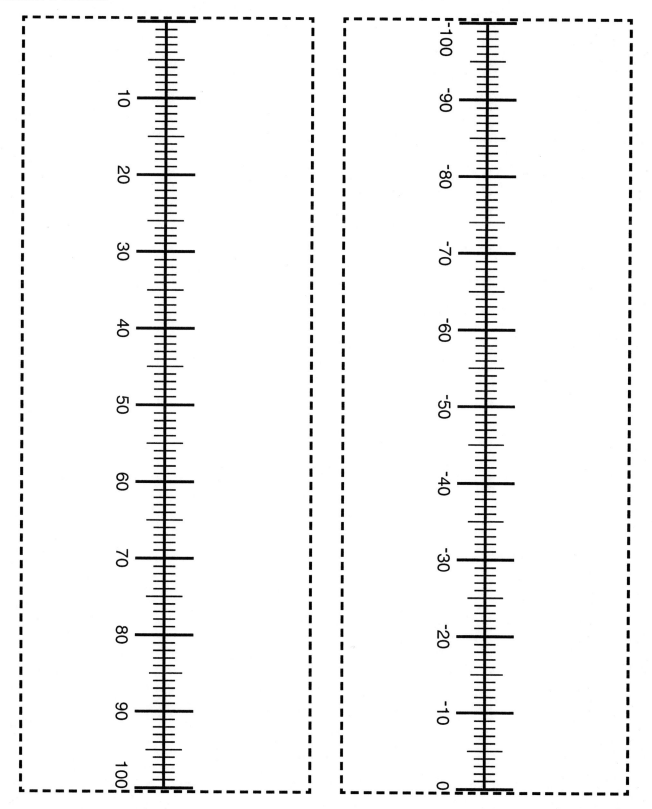

(This page is left blank so you can cut out the manipulatives on the previous page.)

(Esta página está en blanco para permitirle cortar los manipulativos de la página anterior.)

Answer Key

Page 20
1. C
2. K
3. B
4. L

Page 21
1. B
2. B
3. A
4. C
5. D
6. C

Page 22
Answers will vary but should reflect these ideas:

Top: Mrs. Lee and her class are late for the bus.

Bottom: The children enjoyed watching the penguins.

Page 23
1. a. 50
   b. 4th grade
2. a. 98 km
   b. no
3. a. $284.95
   b. yes
4. a. 7
   b. 13
5. a. $3.07
   b. $29.19
6. a. $37.36
   b. $34.64

Pages 24 and 25
Answers will vary.

Page 26
Across:
1. fourteen
3. nineteen
7. seventeen
9. sixteen

Down:
1. fifteen
2. twenty
4. eighteen
5. eleven
6. twelve
8. thirteen

Page 28
1. 1,806,686
2. 858,001
3. 86,311
4. 1,388,647
5. 34,157
6. 1,602,120
7. 2,312,469
8. 405,760

9. 12,938
10. 507,830
11. 43,757

Secret Message: SAY NO TO CALCULATORS!

Page 29
Possible solutions:
1. $6 + 4 - 1 - 2 + 6 + 2 = 15$
2. $9 + 1 - 3 + 1 - 4 + 1 = 5$
3. $9 - 3 + 4 - 1 + 2 + 3 = 14$
4. $5 - 1 + 1 + 3 + 4 + 6 = 18$
5. $9 - 8 + 6 + 3 - 5 + 3 = 8$
6. $2 - 1 + 8 + 9 - 3 + 5 = 20$
7. $5 + 3 + 2 - 4 + 1 + 5 = 12$
8. $4 + 9 + 3 - 7 + 3 - 1 = 11$
9. $7 - 6 + 2 + 8 - 7 - 1 = 3$
10. $9 + 9 - 9 + 2 - 2 - 8 = 1$

Page 32
Answers will vary but should reflect these ideas:
1. Lola
2. loves to watch parrots
3. They are her favorite animals.
4. Lola loves to watch parrots because they are her favorite animals.

Page 33
Answers will vary for the adjectives and adverbs added to each sentence.

Page 34
1. 2,862
2. 900
3. 2,592
4. 1,127
5. 1,242
6. 4,028
7. 1,943
8. 3,510
9. 1,288
10. 6,264
11. 1,729
12. 2,916
13. 8,722
14. 1,462
15. 4,275
16. 1,300
17. 1,288
18. 5,226

Page 35
1. soddy
2. corn dodgers
3. forty niners
4. chips
5. emigrants
6. ague
7. rustlers
8. schooner

Page 36
1. Yes, we go to the library on Tuesday.
2. Mrs. Smith is your teacher.
3. The students in Mr. Garcia's class were reading *Charlotte's Web*.
4. What a wonderful day it is!
5. Jordan, come play with us in Griffith Park.
6. Watch out, Michelle!
7. Maria, what is your favorite kind of math problem?
8. I will paint John's room today.
9. What time is the lunch at Sunset Diner?
10. I got a sticker, a book, and a magazine at Walden's Drug Store.

Page 37

1. 6	2. 12	3. 6
4. 8	5. 9	6. 12
7. 5	8. 12	9. 6
10. 9	11. 7	12. 11
13. 6	14. 9	15. 9
16. 11	17. 7	18. 7
19. 6	20. 6	21. 9
22. 4	23. 11	24. 4
25. 8	26. 7	27. 12
28. 3	29. 11	30. 9
31. 11	32. 12	33. 7
34. 6	35. 7	36. 8

Page 38

I woke up one morning…

I got out of bed…

What a shock I got when…

I ran to my mother…

She said, "It appears those seeds…

Then she looked…

I am feeling better now…

Page 40
1. 15 sq. cm
2. 54 sq. cm
3. 56 sq. in.
4. 70 sq. in.
5. 180 sq. in.
6. 126 sq. in.
7. 99 sq. mm
8. 225 sq. mm
9. 96 sq. cm

Page 41
1. A
2. B
3. A

Page 44
1. S
2. S

Answer Key (cont.)

3. A
4. S
5. A
6. A
7. A
8. S
9. S
10. S
11. A
12. A
13. S
14. S
15. A
16. A
17. S
18. A
19. A
20. S

Page 45

Crossed out sentences:

I got a good grade on my homework assignment, though.

Last week at school I had hall duty.

Our home fireplace uses gas.

I can't remember whether I put plenty of food in my fish tank at home.

My mother says that the fish at our local market do not always seem fresh to her.

Page 46

1. 7
2. 5
3. 2
4. 6
5. 0
6. 9
7. 10
8. 4
9. 14
10. 2
11. 14
12. 19
13. 2
14. 8
15. 10
16. 4
17. 20
18. 10
19. 10
20. 10
21. 3
22. 6
23. 15
24. 20
25. 8
26. 2

Page 47

1. Weather Flash…heavy rains due in an hour.
2. Next on The World Turns… Elizabeth is never seen again.
3. News Extra! A wild horse and deer escape from the zoo.
4. Watch Muscle Man weekly lift weights on channel two.
5. Special Announcement! Ice skating pair wins gold medals.
6. Try a new cereal just for kids! Awesome Oats!

Page 48

Answers will vary.

Page 49

1. 0.31, 0.39, 0.56, 0.75
2. 0.35, 0.37, 0.59, 0.67
3. 1.12, 1.70, 4.78, 6.74
4. 10.04, 35.69, 62.34, 90.22
5. Restful Valley, Raisin City, North Shore
6. Oakland Hills, Crunch Town, Dudley Town
7. Grovertown, St. Barney, North Shore
8. Red River Valley, Dudley Town, North Shore
9. Restful Valley, Oakland Hills, St. Barney
10. Newtonville, Raisin City, St. Barney

Page 50

1. It shocked or scared her.
2. His father got serious and set rules or limits.
3. She was ready to leave.
4. He had not felt well.
5. He slept soundly.
6. He was going to be in trouble.
7. "Stop."
8. "Are you scared, nervous, or changing your mind?"
9. He loves to tell a story.
10. She doesn't know what is happening.

Page 51

1. I
2. E
3. B
4. G
5. C
6. F
7. A
8. H
9. J
10. D

Page 52

1. C
2. E
3. B
4. A

Page 53

1. 9
2. 1
3. 4
4. 4
5. 28
6. 16
7. 4
8. 25

Page 56

1. C
2. K
3. B
4. L

Page 57

1. 33,069
2. 5,922
3. 1,598
4. 864
5. 4,606
6. 2,701
7. 4,930
8. 1,944
9. 1,615
10. 2,128
11. 666
12. 4,094
13. 7,546
14. 4,104
15. 3,225
16. 2,368
17. 3,591
18. 6,384

Page 58

1. responsible
2. understand
3. mean
4. worth
5. material
6. engage
7. aware
8. arrange
9. circle
10. week
11. mountain
12. cycle
13. angle
14. sense
15. Admiral

Page 59

1. D
2. C

Answer Key (cont.)

3. B
4. A

Page 60
1. 18 cm
2. 22 cm
3. 14 in.
4. 28 in.
5. 42 mm
6. 56 mm
7. 22 cm
8. 38 cm
9. 28 in.

Page 61
1. doll's
2. Lena's
3. girls'
4. turtle's
5. Kate's
6. child's
7. boys'
8. penguin's
9. blouse's
10. pan's
11. man's
12. Jen's
13. lions'
14. toys'
15. play's

Page 62
Answer to riddle: How do you make a hot dog stand? Steal its chair.

Page 63
1. D
2. A
3. A

Page 64
1. Uncle Jorge sat on the front porch.
2. I said, "Mom, what I really want to do is to stay home!"
3. My mom and my dad won't be home until 7 p.m.
4. His grandma made a quilt for his birthday.
5. My cousin and my grandma will be coming with my mom.
6. Our grandparents have a surprise for Aunt Aimee.
7. I wrote "Dear Grandma," at the top of my stationery.
8. I wish my aunt lived closer to us; she looks just like Mom.
9. Then Dad stopped and looked behind him.
10. I like to go to Grandmother Norton's house in the summer.
11. My favorite cousin is Jimmy because he makes me laugh.
12. At the wedding we saw Aunt Marsha and Cousin Brad.
13. My mom and dad are taking me to dinner after the awards assembly.
14. At the reunion I saw Aunt Edith, Uncle Jacques, and Cousins Kathy, Meredith, Hector, and Samantha.
15. For my birthday I'm inviting Cousin Sarah, Cousin Leigh, Aunt Susie, and my uncle, whose name is Mike.

Page 65
1. 14, 16, 18, 20, 22
2. 13, 15, 17, 19, 21
3. 16, 19, 22, 25, 28
4. 15, 18, 21, 24, 27
5. 30, 35, 40, 45, 50
6. 35, 42, 49, 56, 63
7. 14, 12, 10, 8, 6
8. 55, 48, 41, 34, 27
9. 70, 50, 40, 30, 20
10. 57, 77, 87, 97, 107, 117
11. 44, 66, 77, 88, 99, 110
12. 32, 64, 128, 256, 512
13. 24, 96, 192, 384, 768
14. 125, 150, 175, 200, 225

Page 68
Chad-Reds

Danny-Cardinals

Andrew-White Sox

Ryan-Dodgers

Will-A's

Page 69
Top: Who or What: representatives from each state except Rhode Island

Did What: met at Constitutional Convention

When: May to August, 1787

Where: Philadelphia, PA

Why: to write the U.S. Constitution

How: by debating and voting

Bottom: What: Transcontinental Railroad

Did What: completed the railroad

When: May 10, 1869

Where: Utah

Why: to let people travel from coast to coast

How: two railroad crews laid tracks starting at each coast

Page 70
1. C
2. A
3. A

4. B
5. B

Page 71
1. B
2. M
3. B
4. L
5. C
6. L

Page 72
1. 103 R3
2. 77 R1
3. 53 R4
4. 106 R1
5. 152 R5
6. 29 R2
7. 13 R5
8. 163 R1
9. 101 R2
10. 104 R3
11. 134 R2
12. 204 R2
13. 228 R3
14. 182 R1
15. 309 R2
16. 190 R1

Page 73
Suggested details to leave out:

Baby animals are cute.

Baby bears are called cubs.

The cubs like to eat honey.

Baby animals must eat.

Baby animals are fun to watch.

Page 75
1. +
2. ÷
3. +
4. −
5. +
6. x
7. x
8. ÷
9. −
10. +
11. x
12. +
13. −
14. +
15. x
16. ÷
17. ÷
18. ÷
19. x
20. x

Answer Key (cont.)

Page 77
1. 13.8 miles
2. 8 miles
3. 15.3 miles
4.–7. Sample answers:
   a. Golf Course to Picnic Area to Lake = 11.7 miles
   b. Golf Course to Cabin to Big City to Lake = 18.2 miles
   c. Golf Course to Camp to Lake = 13.8 miles
   d. Golf Course to Cabin to Big City to Picnice Area to Lake = 22.6 miles
8.–10. Answers will vary depending on routes chosen.

Page 80

Alike: eight years old, best friends, teaching each other their primary language, do homework together, popcorn is favorite snack, love Pete, enjoy the park, play with Pete

Different: Marta doesn't speak English well and Janis doesn't speak Spanish well, Janis has a little brother and Marta has no siblings, Marta is a good skater, Janis has a scooter

Page 81
1. 1/4
2. 3/5
3. 5/6
4. 8/9
5. 2/7
6. 4/9
7. 3/4
8. 5/9
9. 1/3
10. 4/8 or 1/2
11. 2/9
12. 2/8 or 1/4
13. 5/6
14. 4/7
15. 7/9
16. 2/4 or 1/2
17. 3/5
18. 2/3
19. 4/5

Page 83
1. F   6. F
2. O   7. O
3. F   8. O
4. O   9. O
5. F   10. F

Page 84
Example: C
1. B
2. K

3. C
4. L
5. C

Page 85
1. He
2. it
3. She
4. They
5. They
6. her
7. it/him/her
8. He
9. him
10. it
11. It
12. them
13. She
14. her
15. She
16. him
17. We
18. they
19. It
20. They

Page 87
1. F
2. I
3. G
4. D
5. E
6. H
7. L
8. A
9. K
10. M
11. O
12. C
13. B
14. J
15. N

Page 88

A1-white, D3-gray, B4-red, D2-ivory, C4-silver, A2-yellow, D1-black, C2-purple, B3-tan, A4-gold, C3-brown, B1-pink, D4-lavender, B2-green, A3-orange, C1-blue

shaded: A1, A3, B3, C2

striped: B2, C1, C3

unmarked: A2, B1

Page 89
1. A
2. D
3. B